High praise for
DISASTERAMA!
by Alvin Orloff

NO ONE IS cooler than Alvin Orloff, and *Disasterama!* proves it. Orloff's madeleine is Day-Glo, his Balbec the lost queer punk scene in San Francisco at the height of the AIDS crisis. This is memoir in the classic (or classic Hollywood) sense: a witty and glamorous raconteur who's lived a wild life tells all.

> ANDREA LAWLOR, author, *Paul Takes the Form of a Mortal Girl*

ALVIN ORLOFF'S MEMOIR of San Francisco queers facing the mounting AIDS crisis and freaking, caring, denying, performing, and carrying on is a witty remembrance that avoids cheap sentiment or easy responses. Tackling a mass of contradictions with unflinching realness, this book both entertains and inspires.

> MICHAEL MUSTO, columnist, author, *Fork on the Left, Knife in the Back*

DISASTERAMA! TAKES US deep into the 80s and the daily creative resistance that saved the culture's soul during the plague years. With wit and flair Alvin Orloff gives us a guided tour of the era's vibrant subcultures; glittering, pointed reactions to a cold-hearted status quo. Heartbreaking and hilarious, sexed-up and political, *Disasterama!* is a deeply personal coming-of-age story.

> MICHELLE TEA, author, *Against Memoir* and *Modern Tarot*

ALVIN ORLOFF'S *DISASTERAMA!* is a darkly funny memoir depicting SF's Queer Underground during the height of the AIDS Crisis when we were young, angry and horny as hell! This is a remarkable evocation of a heroic time. Long live the queens!!!

> JUSTIN VIVIAN BOND, author, *Tango: My Childhood, Backwards and in High Heels*

ALVIN ORLOFF'S WONDERFULLY detailed elegy to San Francisco's streets and clubs of the 1980s is not your typical AIDS memoir. Orloff and his friends dance, get high, create outrageous art and hustle while their world hovers briefly at the precipice, and then is gone. It is a beautiful remembrance.

> CLEVE JONES, LGBTQ and Labor Activist; author, *When We Rise: My Life in the Movement*

A BOOK THAT all at once reads as a memoir, a eulogy and a love letter to San Francisco—set in those critical years between the death of disco and the first tech boom—*Disasterama!* offers up a chronicle of fags, dykes, punks, freaks, and club kids partying on the Best Coast and the impact of AIDS, art, and activism on the post Baby Boomer/pre-Millennial van garde. SPOILER ALERT: the last three chapters will completely rip yr heart out.

BRONTEZ PURNELL, author, *The Cruising Diaries*

AN IRRESISTIBLE AND seminal work that gives us a glimpse into an explosive era of outspoken and unprecedented art, breathless interpersonal discourse and dysfunction, dug-in protest culture, and mind-bending fashion that put the word "flamboyant" to shame.

RICHARD LORANGER, author, *Sudden Windows*

I'VE NEVER READ a better story of the true love of friendship. Alvin tells the story of the San Francisco I lived in when I first arrived, when all kinds of social misfits and cultural weirdos could call it home. No matter who you were, you could come here and find a place to not only fit in, but to shine.

BUCKY SINISTER, author, *Black Hole*

FILLED WITH SUCH poignant and vivid detail you felt like you lived through it . . . oh wait, I did!

LEIGH CROW, aka Elvis Herselvis

WOW, JUST WOW. *Disasterama!* is the first book and situation that gently explains the life and sociology of a boy and his debating partner, in the grand form of Diet Popstitute, living before the woefully unexplored and common experience of friends, lovers, former lovers, and frenemies dying frequently and fast from the Virus, which took up roughly a decade. I think it was just too hard, fast, and inconceivable, plus a lot of the social talkers were the first to disappear. Do nightclubs change culture? is high culture elitism? glum vs chipper? and how do we talk to the bedridden?—all in this witty saucepan boiler of a book. Stay smart, read *Disasterama!*

—JENNIFER BLOWDRYER, author, *Good Advice for Young Trendy People of All Ages*

DISASTERAMA!

DISASTERAMA!

Adventures in
the Queer Underground
1977–1997

Alvin Orloff

—ɯɯ—

WITH AN INTRODUCTION BY
Alexander Chee

THREE ROOMS PRESS
New York, NY

Disasterama! Adventures in the Queer Underground 1977–1997
BY Alvin Orloff

ACKNOWLEDGEMENTS:
Chapters from *Disasterama!* have been previously published in slightly different form, as follows: "The Doomed Glamor of Polk Street" appeared in *Instant City #6*, Fall 2008; "Nightmare in Hell House" appeared in *Chills, Pills, Thrills, and Heartache* edited by Clint Catalyst and Michelle Tea (Alyson 2004); "Toaster" appeared in *10th & Mission*, Vol. 5; "Anarchy for the USA" appeared in *Specious Species*, Issue # 7; "The Daily Bump 'n' Grind" appeared in *Hos, Hookers, Call Girls and Rent Boys, Professionals writing on Life, Love, Money, and Sex* edited by David Henry Sterry and R. J. Martin Jr. (Soft Skull 2009); "Last Dance" appeared in *Johns, Marks, Tricks and Chickenhawks: Professionals & their Clients Writing about Each Other*, edited by David Henry Sterry and R. J. Martin Jr. (Soft Skull 2013); "Porn Moguls" appeared in *Tricks and Treats: Sex Workers Write About Their Clients*, edited by Matt Bernstein Sycamore (Haworth 2000).

This is a work of creative nonfiction. The events are portrayed to the best of author Alvin Orloff's memory. Some parts of this book, including dialog, characters and their characteristics, locations and time, may not be entirely factual.

ISBN 978-1-941110-82-9 (trade paperback original)
ISBN 978-1-941110-83-6 (ebook)
Library of Congress Control Number: 2019938298
TRP-078

Publication Date: October 8, 2019

BISAC category code
BIO031000 Biography & Autobiography / LGBT
BIO005000 Biography & Autobiography / Entertainment & Performing Arts
BIO026000 Biography & Autobiography / Personal Memoirs
BIO024000 Biography & Autobiography / Criminals & Outlaws

FRONT COVER:
Photo of Alvin Orloff © Daniel Nicoletta: www.dannynicoletta.com

COVER AND BOOK DESIGN:
KG Design International: www.katgeorges.com

DISTRIBUTED BY:
PGW/Ingram: www.pgw.com

Three Rooms Press
New York, NY
www.threeroomspress.com
info@threeroomspress.com

Dedicated to my wonderful siblings, Bo and Ann,
who could save me a lot of embarrassment
if they were to forgo reading this
scandalous memoir of my lunatic youth.

DISASTERAMA!

Introduction

BY ALEXANDER CHEE

THIS BOOK IN YOUR HANDS IS one you could say I've waited for, and I'm not alone. In the year since my own memoir of this time came out, I've heard from so many readers about how they have wanted what it had to offer—and more than that. The era in question, San Francisco in the 1980s and 1990s, was an enormously important time, when the city's culture was under attack by conservative politicians and we saw the birth of the ACT UP and Queer Nation movements.

And when I arrived in San Francisco in 1989, I found the queer punk scene I had not even dared dream of, and the Popstitutes were the hot funny center of that action. Alvin Orloff was their smiling butch. He had a smile that could reach you no matter the mood, and looked like he'd escaped from *The Outsiders*. He's had more life than that, as you'll read here, but it means so much to get the view from the stage, as it were, as well as the life past it. As I learned when I was a go-go dancer, there's nothing like the view you get and with everyone looking at you, they aren't hiding themselves from you. You can really see them, if you look. And he did.

It is ironic to find in these pages the city that has almost vanished under waves of Silicon Valley gentrifiers. I don't know why so much of what happened in the late 80s and early 90s is not online, but it is gradually being written about and archived. It is not the same thing to go to Polk Street now. It is not the same thing to go to the Mission. The stories of those who lived here then and who fought and died for rights we're in danger of losing again, the stories of the rights we still don't have, returned to me as I read this, and I thought of the difference between stories written by those who lived through this and the stories written by those who can only imagine it.

There's a strange love I have for these times that can be hard to explain. How can I love what I lived through from a time that was as "bad" as that? But as I read this, and those days came into view again, what I think of that love now is that there was a beauty to the beauty you found then that was made the more fierce by the horror of what was happening. If you could still find the worth of your life, still find sex, love, friendship, your own self-worth amid these attempts by the state at erasure and the ravages of the AIDS epidemic, then it had the strength of something forged in fire. Queer punk is still with us, still alive, even assimilated by those who would never have dared to support it at the time. Which makes the stories here in *Disasterama!* the more vital. The stories here are not just a simple record but a record of how Alvin faced what he saw and still thrived. There's lessons here if you want them.

So come to the source, as it were. Walk the vanished streets, learn about Go-Go, Harvey Milk, return to a time when neither national political party cared if we lived, much less if we could vote. Learn how making an outfit could be a revolution or at least a call to one. A dream of the future for one night that could become a gift to us all.

—Alexander Chee
JULY 2019

Preface

SOME PEOPLE ARE GOOD IN EMERGENCIES, others less so. My friends and I were Crazy Club Kids, Punk Rock Nutters, Goofy Goofballs, Fashion Victims, Disco Dollies, Happy Hustlers, and Dizzy Twinks. You couldn't count on us to pick up the right carton of milk at the store, let alone file our taxes or remember to take out the trash on Wednesday. We danced with the manic grace of plastic bags caught in the wind, but our bank accounts were empty. We wore clothes that stopped traffic, but few of us knew how to drive. We lived, laughed, and loved like there was no tomorrow, never guessing that for many of us there wasn't. As denizens of what used to be called "The Underground" we were prepared for lives full of social exclusion and unrelenting bohemian squalor. We were not prepared for Acquired Immune Deficiency Syndrome.

It began with newspaper articles full of rare, spooky diseases with unpronounceable names or mysterious acronyms. GRID. Pneumocystis. KS. My friends and I didn't pay attention because, well . . . papers were always full of bad news, right? Then, the rumors started. A friend of a friend of a friend went into the hospital with a cough and never came out. A co-worker's neighbor dropped in his tracks. That guy who was always sitting outside that café? Gone. Still we didn't panic. We were barely into our twenties, so healthy and robust we felt immortal. Our delusions of immunity didn't last long, though. First one friend took ill, then another, then another, then another and another and another. Before long we found ourselves in the midst of a pitiless and unstoppable viral scourge.

As if we didn't have enough problems already, my friends and I!

In those benighted days of yore, wide swaths of the populace believed all homosexuals were degenerates. In our case they were basically right, but—oh!—*they were so mean and judge-y about it.* Everyone I knew was scarred, or at least neuroticized, from family rejection, queer-bashing, or just hearing the bigoted blathering of right-wing politicians and televangelists. Unwelcome in respectable society, we descended into the subterranean lavender twilit shadow world of the gay ghetto. There, in dark clubs and dive bars, we frolicked and reveled, utterly determined to wring every last ounce of pleasure and fun from our wretched lives in what little time we had left.

Meanwhile, the aforementioned politicians and televangelists took an unspeakably irritating "told you so" attitude, loudly proclaiming we gays were getting our just rewards. "AIDS is not just God's punishment for homosexuals," elucidated President Reagan's good friend, Reverend Jerry Falwell. "It is God's punishment for the society that tolerates homosexuals." The resulting climate of paranoid intolerance, along with fear of a rapid and painful death, led many gays to abandon the hallowed traditions of camp humor, arched aestheticism, and sexual anarchy—as if a heapin' helpin' of normalcy might spur the virus and the bigots to leave us all alone. Not so, my friends and I. We doubled down on the queer and assaulted the public with agitprop street theater, drag cabaret, spoken word poetry, performance art, and worse. Our lives became one giant *cri de coeur:* We want to live! And yet, even during this riot of rococo rebellion, we kept dying.

Then, after a decade and a half of terror and trauma, it ended, or slowed down anyway, when the development of protease inhibitor "cocktails" sent the death toll plummeting. The general public (at least outside the Bible Belt) decided it didn't hate gays after all and history marched on to meet its next appointment. The band of merry misfits who'd assembled for mutual support and collective hijinks during the crisis scattered to the winds. People wanted to get on with their lives, not sit around feeling shattered and tragic. A feigned amnesia prevailed across queerdom, albeit one interrupted by brief, sanctioned occasions for dignified mourning.

My dead friends, however, were anything but dignified or mournful. The ghosts of sleazy boys in black leather jackets and cackling queens in tacky frocks nagged me in my dreams. "Hey, Miss Girl! Get off your ass and write something *fun* about us. Nobody else is doing it." Strangely, this appeared to be true. Sure, the heroic crusades of ACT UP and Queer Nation were well and justly remembered, but the swirling, whirling, daffy, and demented fringes of queer social life during the high AIDS era were all but forgotten.

When it comes to publicity, my dearly departed friends are not to be denied. So, to avoid their posthumous pestering, I wrote this book: the true story of how a bunch of pathologically flippant kids floundered through a deadly serious disaster. You can read it as an elegy, apologia, cautionary tale, or social history, but it's also my memoir, and as such it will have to begin with me.

—Alvin Orloff
FEBRUARY 2019

Chapter 1: Polk Street, 1977

A CLOUDLESS EVENING SKY WAS SHADING from deep blue to decadent purple as I stepped off San Francisco's 38 Geary bus and started walking up Polk Street. On the next block I passed a small gaggle of boys—teenagers, like me—loitering outside a head shop with an air of mild insolence. The cutest, a pale, slender kid with a solemn face, took an oversized comb from the back pocket of tight, white jeans and began slowly running it through his shoulder-length dirty-blond hair. He did this with just enough swagger to suggest he might be preening for an audience. Sure enough, I soon spotted a nearby older man staring his way with needy eyes. A frisson of excitement ran up my spine. Once again I'd escaped the drearily heterosexual suburbs for a night in the glamorous gay ghetto, a place where it seemed possible, if only just, that someone would want me for . . . something.

On reaching the popular section of Polk Street, scores of guys were peacocking up and down the sidewalks, perching on cars, and spilling out of bars, all in a state of advanced merriment. A mini-skirted man wearing a ratty orange ladies' wig jumped off the back of an idling motorcycle and ran into a liquor store. A balding, middle-aged Bible-thumper wearing a cheap, brown suit tried to give out tracts but was refused by *everyone*. A pair of guys in tight, shiny, up-to-the-second disco fashions strolled down the street holding hands—*right there in public for all-the-world to see.*

Spotting a few feet of open space in front of Neato Burrito, I leaned against the wall, shoved my hands in my pockets, and tried to look casual. All around, guys were eying each other with a ravenous hunger, flirting, and walking off together. This, I knew (from library research), was the fabled practice of "cruising," a prelude to instant sex. Through careful observation, I discerned three styles: Some guys stared fixedly at their quarry, as if commanding him to come their way by telekinesis. Others tried to make eye contact with every passerby, their head zipping back and forth like spectators at a tennis match. Still others slyly glanced at their prey then quickly looked away, feigning indifference. Too shy for any of these, I stared heavenward with what I hoped was a winsome look on my face and waited.

After what seemed like forever, one of the many cars slowly circling the block pulled to the curb so its driver could ogle me. I was being cruised! Nerves aflutter, I sauntered up to the car just as its passenger door swung open and the man patted the seat next to him invitingly. Like every child in America, I'd been severely warned against getting into cars with strangers. I got in. The man, middle-aged and thus of no interest to me, drove around the block while asking polite questions. How old was I? (Sixteen.) Was I in high school? (Yup, and the kids all wanted to kill me for being a fag.) Did my parents know I was gay? (Yes, and they'd sent me to a shrink.) When we reached the spot where he'd picked me up, the man let me out with a "Nice to meet you." Had he noticed my acne-ravaged face was covered in a virtual mask of Clearasil—a shade of tawny pink that does not, I believe, occur in nature—and been turned off? We'll never know.

My spot in front of Neato Burrito had been taken, so I started walking. The gay part of Polk was six blocks long and after I'd traversed it three times, I decided to try sneaking in somewhere and randomly chose a place called Buzzby's. The club was humid, dark, and tiny—though it looked larger than it was thanks to mirrorized walls. And it was packed with men. On the miniscule dance floor a throng of sweaty bodies writhed under a set of disco lights elaborate enough to put me in mind of an alien spacecraft while Donna Summer boomed from giant speakers, "I feel love, I feel love, I feel looove!" I wiggled my way through the sea of men to the bar and called out to the shirtless, mustachioed bartender. "Excuse me, could I have a beer, please?"

The bartender's lips pursed with suspicion as he peered at me. "Got an ID, sweetie?"

My hand flew theatrically to the pocket of my jacket. "Oh, uh, I think I forgot it at home." The bartender rolled his eyes and turned to help someone else. Humiliated, I fled.

With nothing else to do I walked up the street to Bob's Diner and ordered a soda. As I sat at the counter, I couldn't help but stare at a booth by the front door where five handsome teens sat sharing a single order of fries. The acoustics weren't great, but I was able to eavesdrop just enough to discover they were hustlers! What I knew of gay street life came mostly from John Rechy's lurid 1963 novel, *City of Night,* and "All The Young Dudes," a hyperemotional rock ballad penned by David Bowie for the glam rock band Mott The Hoople. The boys in the booth clearly belonged to the world described in those works: a swirling vortex of petty crime, sexual perversion, illicit drugs, sex-for-sale, and against-all-odds romance.

Despite its glaringly obvious downsides—police harassment, cruel johns, dead-end poverty, and such—I'd have traded that world for my own comfy suburban existence in a heartbeat. Why? The boys! It wasn't just their sizzling sexiness I coveted (though there *was* that), but their camaraderie. Boys such as these surely had nicknames, shared secrets, and slept nude next to other boys. Such boys knew what it was *to be wanted.* As I left the diner I passed right by the hustlers' table. I would've loved to say hello, but years of mockery and bullying at school had left me tongue-tied around strangers. Instead I just flashed a smile that went unnoticed.

Back on the street I resumed my aimless rambles feeling extra-alone and invisible. Night had fallen completely and the street was even more crowded and boisterous than before. Cheerful chatter and flirtatious laughter mingled with traffic noises and the music booming from bars and discos to produce a carnival din. This was no longer just a street, but a raunchy, erotic netherworld, a lusty, boy-packed fever dream lit by the golden glow of street lamps and fueled by yearnings deep and powerful as any holy passion.

* * *

I'D BEEN SPENDING AT LEAST ONE night a week on Polk Street for months and except for the old guy in the car, nobody had so much as glanced my way. I began loitering dolorously outside a place called the The Q.T., not expecting anything but not quite ready for the two long boring bus rides required to get back to my parents' house in Berkeley. After hearing how predatory gays were toward young boys I hadn't expected meeting someone to be so difficult! I was just about ready to give up and catch a bus home when a bartender came out for a smoke break and glanced my way.

"Hey, kid. What's up?"

"Nothing," I said with a full dose of self-pitying teenage petulance. "Absolutely *nothing.*"

"No ID?"

I shook my head. He leaned through the open door to the bar and called out. "Can we do something for this little number here?" Another bartender inside cocked his head indicating for me to go in.

Now, the bar was taking a risk by letting me enter, but not a big one. San Francisco was a party town. Discos stayed open all night, people shared joints on the street, Quaaludes were as common as aspirin, everyone smoked, no one wore sunscreen, and teenagers snuck in everywhere all the time. And while it's true that allowing under-aged boys in a bar was good business if one wanted to attract—*ahem*—a certain clientele, I believe the bartender let me in out of gay solidarity. I was clearly not having fun on the sidewalk and being gay was all about fun. *Fun, fun, fun!* Having been cast out of respectable society and subjected to all manner of cruel persecution, gays felt entitled to compensation in the form of wild parties, cocktail guzzling, dry wit, kinky sex, illegal drugs, high fashion, disco dancing, and the erudite appreciation of old movies and art deco. A fair trade? You tell me.

Inside, the Q.T. was relatively quiet, dark, and furnished with tall stools at tiny tables adorned with those glass-encased candles you see in Italian restaurants. Not wanting to push my luck by ordering a drink, I slunk into a corner and surveyed the clientele: a couple dozen men so generically drab they didn't even look gay. Eventually, a portly fellow in his late twenties wearing business casual clothes and a too-ready smile sidled up to me.

"And what might a little slip of a thing like you be doing in a place like this?"

"Just out for a drink," I said casually, not mentioning my lips had never before touched alcohol. The man held up his index finger indicating for me to wait, went to the bar, and returned with something dark in a glass. I took a sip of what tasted like Coca-Cola and paint thinner. "Thanks."

"My name's Joe. What's yours?" I told him and without waiting a beat he asked, "Like to go somewhere?"

I found Joe unattractive but was determined to lose my virginity before turning seventeen. At that advanced age, I suspected I would no longer qualify as "chicken" and hence be even less desirable than I already was, presuming such a thing were even possible.

"OK."

Before I could take a second sip of the horrible drink, Joe took my hand and pulled me out of the bar. He led me to a cheap hotel a couple blocks down the street and checked us into a room furnished with naught but a saggy bed, ugly brown wallpaper, and a miasma of congealed despair. Joe stripped off his clothes to reveal a blubbery physique. I found my own chubby body repulsive, but next to him I was lithe as

Adonis. As I shimmied out of my own clothes, Joe's eyes glittered lustfully. I'd expected lustful glitter to be warm, but Joe's glitter was cold.

I dove under the covers and, unsure what was supposed to happen next, lay flat on my back and waited. Joe proceeded to ravish me with hand and mouth, pawing and slurping in a manner that suggested he was trying to absorb my youth through osmosis. My body eventually rose to the occasion (if you catch my drift), but my heart and mind were elsewhere. Sex was turning out to be a total yawn. *This?* I thought. *Really? This is what people are so excited about?*

Then—*ouch!*— Joe quickly satisfied his lust at the expense of my virginity. Afterward, I hopped out of bed and quickly pulled my clothes on without any thought of my own gratification. I just wanted to escape the tawdry scene.

"Need bus fare?" asked Joe, his face plastered with a pleased grin.

I didn't, but figured money was money. "Sure." He handed me a couple of bucks. "Thanks."

"See you 'round, Sweet Thing."

"Yeah, bye."

On the interminable bus ride back to my parents' suburban manse, I pondered what had just transpired. In my rush to join the fun, I'd settled for Mr. Wrong. It didn't bother me, really, but I was in no rush to do anything like *that* again.

Chapter 2: Go-Go 1979

A DENSE AND CLAMMY MORNING FOG was burning off to reveal a sky of purest azure. This Gay Freedom Day, like all those before it and all those ever after, would be one of sun-drenched gorgeousness. Bleary-eyed but brimming with enthusiasm, I glanced up and down Spear Street. The cavernous block of the financial district was filled with contingents and party revelers waiting for the parade to begin, with its gaudily dressed marching bands, floats covered with crepe paper or tinsel, drag queens on roller-skates, leather dykes, photographers, and nearly nude men. The year before, at my first parade, I'd been a mere spectator. This time I'd arrived with my own contingent: Go-Gos for Gays.

It wasn't a large contingent—just me and my pals Jennifer Blowdryer, Gwyn, Blackie O., Alexis à Go-Go, and a half-dozen more. We were all outfitted in flashy mid-60s drag: narrow lapelled sports coats and skinny ties for the boys, girls in miniskirts and pointy pumps. For a banner I'd written Go-Gos for Gays in magic marker on a white bed sheet next to which someone had drawn Archie's pals Betty and Veronica dancing in Mod outfits. When our turn to march down Market Street came, I held aloft my tiny portable cassette deck and played a mix-tape of my favorite Go-Go hits: the Zombies, the Troggs, Petula Clark. Unfortunately the crowd couldn't hear this because directly behind us a gigantic motorized float from some bar was blasting Sister Sledge's "We Are Family" on an endless loop while bodybuilders in sequined short-shorts did that little stepping-flexing dance guys do when they can't move much because their muscles are so huge. My group, by contrast, danced down the street like kids in a Beach Party movie doing the Twist, Swim, and Watusi. When the crowd—guestimated at 200,000—noticed us at all, they looked confused, so we began chanting, "Twist! And shout! And shout it on out! We're Go-Gos! For Gays! Go-Gos! For Gays!"

At the corner of Market and Powell a mystified reporter shoved a mic in my face. "Go-Gos for Gays? What's this all about?"

"We're promoting awareness of Go-Go music from the 1960s!" I chirped. "The Beau Brummels! Lesley Gore! The Searchers! The Shangri-Las!"

"Where does the gay come in?"

I tried to think. "Uh . . . We like gays!"

The reporter nodded and wandered off wearing an *Oh, brother* look.

We reached the parade's terminus at Civic Center around noon. My compatriots went home to nap (none of us were morning people), but I stuck around to mingle with the mob in the hopes of finding romance. Alas, my fellow gays were already in boozey-cruisey mode, shedding shirts and inhibitions faster than you can say *voulez-vous coucher avec moi?* I

wandered about for hours, but this was a festival of the flesh—
my Beatle Boots and polka-dot tie impressed no one.
Eventually I gave up and went home.

* * *

MY FIXATION WITH GO-GO HAD BEGUN a couple years previously when I started shopping for vintage clothing at thrift
stores. There, in addition to the usual bargain hunters, I
encountered Retro Queens. Unlike Antique Queens, who collected tasteful, high-quality *objets* to shield their delicate
sensibilities from the vulgarity of the modern world, Retro
Queens collected *démodé* kitsch to shield their indelicate sensibilities from the tedium of Good Taste. They were high
priests of camp, enthusiastically venerating the sort of pop
culture debris that could be bought for next-to-nothing
because affluent, well-educated people found it repulsively
vulgar. "My God, it's faaabulous!" they'd shriek on finding a
boomerang ashtray, Tiki-themed cocktail set, *Flying Nun* lunch
box, black velvet clown painting, or a set of pink plastic
Melmac dinnerware.

It impressed me to no end that *everything* the Retro Queens
did came with a heapin' helpin' of *sparkle*. Ask an average
person how your second-hand Daffy Duck tee shirt looks and
he'll shrug and say, "OK." Ask a Retro Queen, and he'll arch
his eyebrow and tilt his head appraisingly before gushing,
"Oh, *Dollface*, that shirt is *faaabulous*! It lifts and hugs and sup-
ports in *all* the right places. Don't you *dare* even *think* about
not buying it." The implications of such extravagant behavior
were clear: all clothing is costume because life is theater and
it's your job to steal every scene so you can become a STAR . . .
or at least a good character actress.

To me this looked like jolly good fun and, as an added bonus, it felt deliciously forbidden. Thanks to my lefty egghead family, I'd grown up believing Americans were brainwashed automatons obsessed with getting ahead in the rat race so they could keep up with the Joneses and pave over paradise while bombing this or that country back to the Stone Age. All entirely true, of course, but now I saw that Americans could also be appealingly weird. After all, their much-lamented obsessions with technology, artifice, and Pollyanna optimism had respectively produced the Moog Synthesizer, Jayne Mansfield, and the It's a Small World ride at Disneyland. Americans weren't *completely* bad! People afflicted with good taste—it seemed to me—lived in a defensive cringe, while campy queens were free to embrace the flawed and farcical world around them with open arms.

Retro Queens tended to specialize in something particular: Rockabilly, Beatniks, Film Noir, Mid-Century Modernism, the Rat Pack, creepy dolls, or what have you. I never had to consider my choice. I was magnetically attracted to Go-Go, an amalgam of 1960s fads, styles, and happenings with special focus on Warhol's Factory, Swinging London, and the preposterous simulacrums of youth culture found on TV (*The Monkees*, say, or Cousin Serena from *Bewitched*). I read Jackie Susann's overwrought novel of showbiz pill-poppers, *Valley of the Dolls*, collected Margaret Keane prints of bathetically big-eyed children, perused old magazines to gape at Space Age fashions or early rumblings of the sexual revolution, and spent endless hours watching giddily madcap films like *Barbarella* or *Wild in The Streets*.

At first this was all done ironically, with an eye to the giggle, but irony is an unstable compound. Over time, it breaks down into a complex mixture of facetiousness and sincerity, allowing for all sorts of nuance. It becomes, in a word, fascination. This was especially true with me and Go-Go because it aligned (in my mind, if nowhere else) with secular humanism, left-utopian politics, artistic iconoclasm, and the sort of militant flippancy favored by high-spirited youngsters who really know how to have a good time. Thus, although I was a moody teen, I always tried to act super-perky and behave as if crashing a wild party—one of those groovy "Now Generation" Happenings full of far-out fashions, wisecracking, bikinis, martinis, and strobe lights.

I don't know if people *always* become what they pretend to be, but I certainly did. And, as an unanticipated result, my baseline emotional state reset from Glum to Chipper. This transformation felt nothing short of miraculous, and Go-Go became my *de facto* religion, the mystico-philosophical frame-work I relied on to provide life-guidance and console me in times of trouble. When overwhelmed by romantic loneliness, I listened to Girl Groups whose hilariously over-the-top lamen-tations made the very concept of heartbreak seem amusingly kitsch. When mocked or beaten up for being "a fucking faggot" by my peers, I found solace in the adoration of David Bowie, who was clearly some sort of saint or deity who'd fallen to Earth in order to repeal all gender norms. And when the sheer dullness of life got me down, I'd frug and twist around my room till I felt nothing but *up, up, up.*

My Go-Go worldview faced its first severe test in November 1978 when Dan White shot Harvey Milk, the most visible face of the Gay Rights movement. The assassination left me utterly gobsmacked. For months I read every story in every paper trying to comprehend the horror. After White got off with a wrist slap seven-year sentence, I heard a lady on the bus defending him because "the gays have gone too far." I'd known most straight people didn't *like* homosexuals. I hadn't realized so many wanted us dead. This was scary and annoying, sure, but also thrilling. Being disliked is a wishy-washy experience compared to being homicidally detested.

Thrilling or not, I had to fit the reality of belonging to a despised minority into my flippant worldview. I did this by developing the conceit that I was Glamorously Doomed. My life was a comedy, but a black comedy. My enemies, a category I perceived as consisting of, but not restricted to, right-wingers, sports enthusiasts, and the religiously inclined, were the antagonists required of any good drama. Likewise, my troubles and travails were simply necessary plot complications. Me? I was the hilariously ill-fated protagonist: broke, homely, and afflicted with an artistic temperament, but not endowed with any discernable talent. I was born to lose. And yet by losing *glamorously*—dressed to the nines with a quip on my lip—I would actually win. Like the debris Retro Queens snapped up in thrift stores to repurpose as vintage collectables, the magic of camp would transform *me* into something of value. Being Glamorously Doomed meant I could revel in my own disgrace, laugh in the face of failure, and wear society's scorn like a feather boa. I might be destined for disaster, but my disasters would be *faaabulous!*

Chapter 3: 1979: The Manly, Manly Clones of Castro Street

I NEVER WENT BACK TO POLK Street after that first, fateful pick-up, but a couple years later, I decided to try my luck elsewhere. By that time I'd graduated high school, moved to the city to attend San Francisco State, and was living in a squalid flat full of kids a mere mile away from the Castro, land of the Clones. Conventional wisdom had it the Castro Clones were rejecting the disempowering stereotype of the "Sissy" and reclaiming their masculinity: that the whole conflation of male-on-male love with effeminacy was a mistake based on 19th century pseudo-science and from now on the archetypical gay man would be a "Manly Man." As a result of this thinking, the Castro resembled an open-air costume ball where everyone had decided to dress as either the Brawny Paper Towel Man or one of the Village People. This masquerade of manliness was not just ubiquitous, but mandatory. Clone sentiment toward non-Clones was summed up by the (allegedly) comical tee shirt slogan "No mustache, no banana." Femme guys were about as popular as women, and in 1978 they actually outlawed drag at the gay parade.

I arrived in the Castro on a typical San Francisco summer evening, chilly and foggy, but everyone was dressed for heat. Lumberjack shirts were unbuttoned to reveal chiseled torsos, tee shirts were sleeveless to display bulging biceps, and shorts were cut high to showcase muscular thighs. All Clones were The Strong Silent Type, so there was none of Polk Street's carnivalesque sparkle. Cruising was a *serious* business on Castro, not an occasion for giggling or screaming out "Hey girlfriend!" I desperately hoped one of these creatures might be so indiscriminately randy he'd give me a try. But, there I was, in my utterly wrong outfit: Beatle boots, black peg-leg jeans and mint green button-down shirt, Clairol blue-black hair, and my usual full face of make-up.

Oh, have I not mentioned the make-up? Well, it started in high school when I gave up trying to cure my horrendous acne with Clearasil and started hiding it with foundation. I could never find a shade to match my fair-but-blotchy skin and wound up looking rather wan and pasty. This necessitated subtle blush to liven my cheeks and a hint of lipstick. My eyebrows were already dyed black to match my hair, so, to make my lashes match, I gobbed on black mascara, which quite naturally demanded eyeliner, which then begged for a little eye shadow. Despite how this sounds, I was *not* exploring what we now call Gender Issues. I felt fey, but still 100 percent boy. Besides, my make-up didn't make me look girly, but more like synth-pop superstar Gary Numan.

After a few small eternities of being ignored while watching the Clones around me hook up with breathtaking speed and ease, I grew bored and started peeking into bars. In every one, I saw guys posing like macho mannequins while their eyes scanned the crowd with robotic efficiency for attractive male flesh. There wasn't a lot of chat, which made sense to me. If you're just going to hop in bed with someone then leave and hop in bed with someone else, why waste time with socializing? So many men, so little time! This compulsive style of cruising wasn't confined to the bars. All around were gay barbershops, gay restaurants, gay laundromats, gay *everything*, and in all these places the Clones cruised and cruised and cruised.

Eventually I spotted a fellow youngster loitering seductively next to a gay lamppost in front of a gay hardware store. He was extraordinarily ordinary with a forgettable face, medium blah hair, and a nothing outfit. His selling point for me was that, unlike every other male within a ten-block radius, he didn't sport a mustache (I really didn't care for mustaches). As I steeled myself to walk over and say hello, my palms grew clammy, my pulse raced, and my feet froze.

"He's just a guy," I told my feet. "What's the worst that could happen?"

My feet remained firmly in place.

"Forward march!" I commanded.

No dice.

I tried humor. "Feets get movin'!"

Nada.

"Look," I reasoned, "Someone has to make the first move. Maybe he's shy."

My feet remained unmoved.

I broke down and whined, "Is it a crime to say hello? Am I not a human being? We're in the middle of a sexual revolution yet I remain trapped in the Bastille of chastity. Why are you destroying my life? Have pity on me!" My feet were having none of it. Realizing I was licked, I gave up and shuffled home to my empty, empty room.

Determined to try, try again, I began going to the Castro a few times a week to stand around. Usually I was invisible, but sometimes clones took time out of their busy erotic schedules to glare disapprovingly at my outfits. Once, a Clone with crazy, coked-out eyes actually spat on me! Eventually, in desperation, I tried butching up. Being eighteen, I felt I could still pull off a juvenile delinquent look and donned tight jeans, a black tee shirt, and black Converse All Stars, then greased my hair into a Rockabilly waterfall. Nobody glared at my outfit, but nobody said hello either. In my heart of hearts, I ultimately didn't care for several reasons, mostly having to do with the aforementioned mustaches.

First, in my mind, mustaches were inextricably linked to adulthood, a condition I associated with home mortgages, light jazz, auto insurance, decrepitude, and death. Second, mustaches reminded me of barbershop quartets, which I have never enjoyed. Third, I felt unshakably certain that the proper accessory of choice at that moment was not the mustache, but the skinny tie. Fourth, the Clones' uniformity revealed a herd-like disrespect for the hallowed tradition of expressing individuality through fashion. Fifth, the theatrical masculinity of the Clones reeked of *trying too hard,* indicating a level of insecurity that belied the very masculinity they were so intent on broadcasting. The Clones' butch posturing looked to me like nothing more than ego assertion and emotional rigidity camouflaged in flannel and denim. Butch guys wasted so much psychic energy suppressing what they perceived as feminine in themselves (their vulnerable, nurturing, creative sides) they became enervated shells: virile and masculine outside, fearful and self-loathing inside.

Was I angry at the Clones? Well, yes. And yet, I also admired them . . . a bit, anyway. Their homogeneity was creepy, but it also made them super-visibly gay, which annoyed all the keep-it-hidden homophobes. When Dan White got his minimal sentence for shooting Harvey Milk, the Clones massively rioted outside City Hall, sending a clear message that from now on queer bashing had consequences. *Go Clones!* And there was definitely a playful aspect to the Clones' masculinity. I mean, how seriously can one take grown men who walk around in cut-off short-shorts with mirrored sunglasses and yellow hard-hats? And, in all fairness, a lot clones were plenty campy when not cruising, enjoying old movies and worshipping divas like any good gay.

On some level I knew the time of the swishy, sissy fairy (the gay archetype with which I identified) was over. Sure, there would always be effeminate men, but the theatrical amplification of feminine traits as a means of broadcasting sexual preference was obsolete. I took solace in the realization that the sissy's greatest spiritual consolation and most potent weapon—the camp sensibility—would live on. More and more hip straight people were imbibing camp's *glamtastic* cocktail of amoral aestheticism, scathing wit, and the erudite appreciation of schmaltz. The queer lisp might die out, but there would always be people who found the earnest and mundane shriekingly funny.

Back to the Castro. After a few weeks I admitted to myself what I'd known from the start: Castro Street was not for me. I gave up going out all together and spent my nights at home, moping and whining. Most everyone is terrified of at least one thing beyond all reason: spiders, poverty, cancer . . . something. My greatest fear was solitude. Was I destined to sit alone in my room forever, unloved and forgotten by humanity? I was beginning to think so when I got wind of a development with the potential to change everything.

Chapter 4: Meet Michael

IT WAS THE BEST NEWS I'D heard in all my miserable eighteen years: On Monday nights a gay bar was going to start spinning new wave! A radio-friendly spin-off from punk, new wave combined a mood of stylish alienation with danceable pop beats and theatrical flair. Serious Thinkers and punk purists reviled it as insipid commercial dreck, but I didn't care. New wave was fun, often campy, and fast becoming the music of choice for young gay weirdoes and misfits—the music we put on the stereo to remind ourselves that we were right and the world was wrong. A bar playing new wave was exactly the right place for me to find a boyfriend.

Monday night I spent two solid hours trying on everything in my closet before settling on a blue-and-black checkerboard dress shirt, a skinny orange tie with black polka dots, black peg-leg jeans, and red Converse sneakers. I slathered my face with foundation to cover my acne, gobbed black mascara on my lashes so they'd match my Lady Clairol blue-black hair, and smudged kohl around my eyes for added mystery. Then I went to the kitchen and inveigled my best friend and roommate

Jennifer into coming along as my security blanket and wingman, the latter a role for which she was perfectly suited.

Stunningly pretty and partial to leopard print, spiky heels, and bleached hair, Jennifer looked like one of the Gabor sisters gone punk, and was, in fact, the lead singer of her own band, The Blowdryers. Gay men invariably adored her on sight and, once they got a load of her campy sensibility, worshipped her. Together we tromped down to the South of Market neighborhood where, on a desolate street full of closed auto repair shops and brick warehouses, we found and entered The Stud.

Being underage, we furtively slunk past the bar without buying drinks and settled against the back wall. The Stud's dark, wood-paneled interior made it look like an Old West Saloon, but one in which the cowboys and gold miners had been magically replaced by new wave hipsters, glitter queens, gay punks, underground artists, hippie holdovers, beat poets, madwomen, and a smattering of unclassifiable oddballs—people who, when they finished putting on clothes, were not merely "dressed" but "working a look." I had no doubt that each and every denizen of this depraved demimonde lived a life of fearless and noble eccentricity. And they were all having *such* a good time! People threw their heads back and cackled like maniacs, hoisted their cocktails with piratical heartiness, swished about with femme fatale belligerence, and danced with anarchic abandon to the best music ever: Siouxsie and the Banshees, XTC, Gang of Four, Joy Division, and the Flying Lizards.

Jennifer and I had been loitering for perhaps half an hour when a poetically thin and prodigiously freckled redhead leaning at the bar caught sight of us. Raising his thin eyebrows in a theatrical greeting, he strode our way with a bouncing gait. His outfit—tattered jeans with huge cuffs, a hole-y striped tee shirt, and a disintegrating black vinyl jacket held together with silver electrical tape—impressed me to no end by looking at once confidently bohemian and adorably little boyish.

"Hey, I'm Michael. You're Jennifer Blowdryer. I saw your band play at the Mabuhay. Great show. I love that Farfisa organ, it's so '60s."

"Thanks," said Jennifer.

"I'm Alvin," I volunteered.

Michael glanced at me. "Oh, hi." He turned back to Jennifer. "So, when are you going to play again?"

For the rest of the evening, Michael did his best to entertain and enchant Jennifer, serving up compliments and flattering questions along with witticisms, grousing, and gossip. As he spoke, I marveled at his eyebrows, which were always arching, furrowing, or wiggling so as to offer meta-commentary on whatever blarney came out of his mouth. He almost didn't even need to speak; all by themselves his eyebrows cracked jokes, made acerbic comments, and recited blank verse. (If this sounds implausible, please note that Leonard Bernstein once used only his eyebrows to conduct Haydn's *Symphony No. 88* in a live performance by the Vienna Philharmonic.) On learning Jennifer and I were teens, Michael—fully legal at twenty-one— bought rum and Cokes for us. When the B-52s came on, he jumped around the dance floor with us. When the night ended, he invited himself home with us. Then, once inside our flat, Michael turned to me with a be-dimpled smile and put his hand on my shoulder. "Which way's your bedroom?"

I couldn't have been more shocked if I'd stuck a wet finger in a light socket. My heart raced and thudded wildly as we fell onto my single, unmade bed. Michael's skin felt silky warm and he smelled like playing in the backyard on a sunny summer day. Then he kissed me and I saw stars. Explosions. Implosions. Transmogrifications. Fireworks. The Earth moved, time grooved, and I fell through a crack in the space-time continuum to find myself *inside* an imaginary David Bowie song, a lost track from the Ziggy Stardust album all about Michael and me and our cosmic communion.

After making out for a while, we began trying to fold part A into slot B and such, but nothing quite fit anywhere. As I fought off waves of self-recrimination and panic (wasn't *the first time* supposed to be magical?), Michael got out of bed and found his jacket lying on the floor. He produced a pint of bourbon from the pocket, took a long swig, and held it out my way. "Want some?" Unused to hard liquor, I took a tiny sip and handed it back. "Thanks." Michael rejoined me on the bed and began talking. Over the next hour I learned he'd grown up in a working class Irish Catholic family, to whom he wasn't "out." Mom cashiered at a supermarket and Dad worked nights as a mechanic at the gigantic GE plant straddling his hometown, Pittsfield, Massachusetts. "Appropriately named 'cause it's the pits," averred Michael. He'd suffered all the usual gay persecution and had to get around town crawling through shrubbery and ducking behind parked cars like a spy.

Michael had been about to board a Greyhound for the start of his second year at U Mass when, on a whim, he'd switched buses. He arrived in San Francisco carrying only his dad's

WWII duffel bag stuffed with clothes, and settled into the National Hotel, an ancient and decrepit red brick SRO on Market Street. He found a job selling porn at a store in North Beach on Broadway near the Condor: a club notorious for its gigantic sign depicting a bikini-clad Carol Doda, queen of the topless dancers, with flashing red lightbulb nipples. Then, he took up poetry.

"Really?" I found this shocking. Who wrote poetry?

"I was into Jim Carroll and Patti Smith, so I bought some yellow legal pads and just started churning it out." Michael's eyebrows indicated he was being sardonic and modest. "It was about losing faith in church and state, the city's squalid underbelly, the horrors of human perfidy, Beatnik-y stuff like that." I wondered what perfidy meant but was loathe to interrupt his flow by asking. "I didn't know what do with my poems, so I'd stand outside bars at last call to read them. I was not a smash hit so I gave it up and started hanging out at the Mabuhay where I saw your friend Jennifer."

I managed to interject the first bit of my own bio: atheistical leftwing half-Jewish family, bookworm, and aspiring writer of comical essays—but before I got any further Michael yawned and rolled onto his side. "Well, g'night." His breathing quickly grew slow and regular. He was sleeping. For a long while I lay perfectly still, so smitten I could barely breathe. Eventually, I molded my body against his and drifted off. The next morning, I rose gingerly so as not to disturb the sleeping beauty beside me and tiptoed to the kitchen to fix English muffins. When I came back, Michael was stretching himself awake. He cast a bleary glance at my alarm clock. "I should go." As Michael threw on his clothes, I scribbled my number for him on slip of paper. He thrust it into his jeans pocket and gave me a little wave. "Later." As he clomped down the front stairs, I wondered if he'd call.

Michael did call. And call and call and call. At first, he did most of the talking, lecturing me on European cinema, existentialism, Stephen Sondheim, radical labor history, German expressionism, glam rock, and similar arcana. Eventually I began talking back and we got into a series of unresolvable debates. Was Franz Marc a great painter? Was US entry into WWII justified? Were the Monkees really better than the Archies? After a few of our epic gabfests my six roommates jointly demanded I quit monopolizing our shared telephone, so I started hanging out at Michael's place.

Everything about the National fascinated me, from the 300-pound mannish leather dyke at the front desk to the communal bathrooms (ick!), to the mysterious residents—down-and-outers, new-to-towners, and suspicious characters who looked like they might be "on the lam." Michael's room was miniscule, so eventually we'd sally forth into the city to drink at dive bars, eat greasy Chinese food, shop at thrift stores, dance at clubs, crash parties, see bands, or just roam the streets from dusk till dawn, both of us always talking, talking, talking.

Often as not, our conversation devolved into airy persiflage.

Example #1: Say that anti-gay demagogue Anita Bryant let loose in the press with another "homosexuals will destroy civilization" tirade. Me: "She might be right. Bonds of male loyalty—team spirit, party affiliation, and nationalism—feed on sublimated homosexual longing. Desublimate it and men will unbond, plunging society into a war of each against all." Michael: "Which would actually be quite refreshing. Western Civilization is becoming intolerably repetitive. We've had so many wars they're not even naming them any more, just giving them numbers. World War One, World War Two . . . It's like they're not even trying."

Example #2: Say we hear someone playing new wave pretty boy Adam Ant's cover of the Doors' song, "Hello I Love You." Me: "Adam Ant has made Jim Morrison redundant." Michael: "No, the Doors are unique, though they should only be listened to while driving ninety miles an hour on the L.A. freeway in a big American car after midnight." Me: "You can imagine Adam Ant kissing himself in the mirror, but not Jim Morrison. Why? Adam Ant is aware of his own narcissism, Morrison wasn't." Michael: "That 'know thyself' business is overrated. Boys wrapped in a cocoon of self-delusion are much sexier."

Within a month of our meeting, Michael and I were best buddies. We never slept together again after that first night (to my great disappointment). I was not, apparently, Michael's type. What his type was I didn't know, as he kept his love life shrouded in mystery. With Michael's coaching I managed to date a couple guys but couldn't get serious about either of them because I found men who weren't Michael deadly boring. I thought that since we were obviously soulmates we should be lovers too, but whenever I brought it up (probably twice a week at least), Michael laughingly poo-poohed the idea. By my reckoning, that didn't really matter. We were a pair of merry malcontents, a dynamic duo, a conspiracy of two, and I was certain we'd never, ever part.

Then, one pale, gray February afternoon a year-and-a-half after we'd met, Michael phoned with some news. "I'm moving to New York."

"What?"

"My plane leaves tomorrow."

Vertigo. Dizziness. Terror. "But *why?*"

"I'm bored."

Chapter 5: New York, New York

A FEW LONELY MONTHS AFTER MICHAEL departed, I
dropped out of school, quit my messenger job, and said goodbye to friends and family so I could join him in Manhattan.
Arriving in the June of 1981, I settled into town with plenty of
gusto, but no *savoir-faire*. Utterly lacking in experience, skills,
or stick-to-itiveness, I got—then lost or quit—a series of menial
jobs in record time: mail room clerk, bicycle messenger, bath-
house attendant. You couldn't sink any lower. As for living
quarters, Michael and I shared a studio on West 14th Street, a
gang and graffiti-ridden boulevard of broken dreams. Our
building was in some sort of renovation limbo and not strictly
supposed to be inhabited so there was no heat, but it did have
a loft bed, which I thought terribly chic.

Most every evening Michael and I popped pills—black
beauties, Christmas trees, white crosses—then hit the bars for
booze and chatter. New Yorkers have always been a garrulous
lot, and even in the lowest dives people held forth on art, politics, and their homespun philosophies, along with the
perennial gay topics of which famous people were secretly gay

and where all the hot boys were. When, thanks to the pills, we started feeling tingly and superhuman we'd head off to Danceteria where we'd dance to the likes of Soft Cell, O.M.D., Heaven 17, Altered Images, Taco, Fad Gadget, Depeche Mode, Duran Duran, Scritti Polliti, Pigbag, and Yaz.

Michael, always looking for social significance, ascribed world-historical importance to our nightlife. "Nightclubbing is recreation, and recreation allows us to *re-create* ourselves *and* society," he proclaimed. "It's easy to tune out the disadvantaged when they're chanting slogans and waving protest signs. But at nightclubs, everyone's guard is down and they'll listen to strangers who've led lives different from their own and learn to see them as human. You can change people's opinions faster with stories than debates. For example, Gilded Age plutocrats only socialized with their own kind so they didn't see the working class as human. Then, in the Roaring Twenties with Café Society, it became hip to socialize with writers, gangsters, flappers, artists, actors, and musicians. The rich learned to see their social inferiors as fun, interesting characters and consequently developed sympathy for them. That breakdown in snobbery helped make the New Deal possible when the depression hit. And after interracial socializing became popular with Beats and on the jazz scene in the 1950s, it became *de rigueur* for whites to support civil rights. Now that straight people socialize with gays at discos and new wave clubs it won't be long before supporting gay rights becomes so hip only total bumpkins will dare be homophobes."

In 1981, gay male sleaze reached an all-time apex. Gay New York was a non-stop erotic cabaret, a raunchy netherworld of bathhouses and bars with back rooms, streets full of cruisers, and parks full of perverts. Plenty of guys were monogamous, sure, but the prevailing mood celebrated promiscuity and sexual specialization. There were guys obsessed with black leather, orgy rooms, hustlers, muscles, the piers, bondage, transvestites, glory holes, exhibitionism, "chicken," you name it and the more the merrier. In San Francisco, Michael had been nearly asexual, but in New York, he became a dedicated horndog. Since I accompanied him everywhere, I suddenly found myself in *all sorts* of sexy places and quickly discovered that something was seriously different. In switching coasts I'd gone from invisible to irresistible! Men ogled me, introduced themselves, bought me beers, and invited me home. These men, I understood, were not interested in me as a person. They barely listened to a word I said, undressed me with their eyes, and invaded my space with octopus arms. For them I was a trophy or a boytoy, a mere object existing solely for their own lurid, sexual gratification.

Finally!

I gleefully went home with man after man and frequented back rooms where I enjoyed a smorgasbord of fleshly delights. In this slutty milieu every sexual encounter was infinitely casual, an act without an echo. And yet, for me, these acts never resembled the soulless athleticism of porn. While surrendering to physical pleasure my babbling brain shut up and my sense of self dissolved. I felt—*don't laugh*—a profound sense of mystical communion with the soul of humanity and a transcendent love for the cosmos.

Well, that, and the cheap ego gratification of being found attractive. Cheap or not, such gratification changed me. Growing up as a sexually-frustrated youth I'd regarded my body as a shameful and disappointing nuisance, a thing to be managed and hidden under clothing. Once I'd joined the ranks of the doable, I saw my body as man-bait, something to be displayed and wielded—a thing, albeit one I was happy to own. Then, slowly, over the course of a thousand kisses and caresses, my psyche conjoined with my flesh. My body became *me* and I became a *boy animal*, someone who might just climb a tree for fun, walk atop a fence balancing like a cat, or run about half naked enjoying the feel of sun and wind on my skin.

While romping about New York I discovered two facets of gay life that became leitmotifs of my young adulthood: gender-bending and hustling. First contact with both came via another pair of inseparable friends, Vinny and Jade. Vinny, who worked with Michael at a dirty movie theater on West Street, was a tough, wiry kid with a scrunchy little face, but cute. He spoke in the profanity-laden patois favored by New York's outer-borough underclass. "So fuckin' hot out dere ya could fry a egg on a bald man's head!" Around him I felt like Little Lord Fauntleroy. Vinny's employment at the theater was temporary as his preferred occupation was hustling. He was renowned for his ability to pick up tricks anywhere—in line at the bank, riding the subway—and told dramatic stories that imbued him with Wild Boy Outlaw allure. He'd had to quit hustling when an over-enthusiastic customer accidentally damaged his nether-regions, but as soon as he saved up enough for some unspecified operation, he planned to quit the theater and return to the big money and glamor of selling his ass.

Jade was a delicately thin queen with a long face, sharp cheekbones, and big teeth—like a horse crossed with a supermodel. I say queen, but Jade's gender was blurry. If pressed, I'd say she was 20 percent effeminate gayboy, 20 percent drag queen, 20 percent transvestite, and 40 percent transsexual. Jade sewed her own outfits of the so-wrong-they're-right variety which she paraded around in everywhere, even drearily dangerous West Street where truckers and men from New Jersey went for closet-case sex. After seeing her in a purple satin leotard with a short cape I wondered aloud if she weren't tempting fate. New York, like absolutely everywhere, was full of queer-bashers who mocked, robbed, beat, bludgeoned, and occasionally killed their targets.

"She'll be OK," Michael assured me. "Street queens are tough. They *have to* be. Remember, it was queens who fought the police at Stonewall back in '69."

On Tuesdays, Jade, Vinny, Michael, and I always went to the Anvil for new wave night. Located in an ancient brick building on the edge of the meatpacking district, the club was notorious for raunch. Connoisseurs of decadence, like German film director Rainer Werner Fassbinder (in full leather) and Truman Capote (allegedly), went there to gape at nude go-go boys, dance with abandon, or join the throngs of beautiful men in the basement who were (as the joke went) engaged in their own brand of meatpacking. The club also hosted drag acts like the seven-foot-tall Euba who—perhaps taking the epithet "flaming faggot" a bit too literally—often livened up her songs' finales by setting herself on fire.

When, after much trying, Jade got herself booked at the Anvil, Vinny, Michael and I stood in front of the stage to cheer her on as she lip-synced "Atomic," a danceable torch/anthem by Blondie. On reaching the lyrics, "Oooooh, your hair is beautifuuuul!" Jade knelt down to Michael and lovingly tousled his locks—recently bleached arctic white—while he gazed up at her in starry-eyed rapture. This wasn't a man in a dress aping femininity for laughs, but a solemn ritual in which an androgyne priestess channeled goddess energy for her audience of congregants. Raised by devout atheists, I'd never felt the slightest twinge of religiosity, but that night I joined the cult of gay Diva worship.

The worst thing about New York was its high cost of living. My paltry paychecks barely got me through each week, plus Michael had a habit of borrowing money and not paying it back. In desperation, I decided to become a gold digger, which *actually made sense!* Like all good gays, I'd spent countless hours watching movies from Hollywood's Golden Age, swooning over sassy starlets who overcame adversity with moxie, pizzazz, and a ready supply of snappy one-liners. As a result, my subconscious was crowded with doddering dowagers, scheming chorus girls, and madcap heiresses. To these gals, becoming a gold digger seemed a perfectly natural career choice. So yes, my morals were deranged, but don't blame me! Blame Fox, Warner, RKO, Paramount, and MGM.

I didn't quite manage to marry a millionaire, but I did snag Spencer, a tiny, balding, bespectacled lawyer in his late twenties. He wore nice Armani suits, lived in a swank West Village apartment, and his cheeks dimpled cutely when he smiled. Also in his favor, Spencer introduced me to the music of Nino Rota and the new East Village art scene. Unlike sugar daddies in the movies, though, Spencer failed to shower me with diamond bracelets or rent me a swank apartment. Still, he did pay my way into chic clubs and take me out to dinner a lot. It helped.

We'd been dating a couple of months when Spencer's gay and *Teen Beat*-ishly handsome little brother, Brendan, showed up. I would've found him attractive except that he dressed like a boring Preppie and radiated a slick, cold air of blasé entitlement. An aspiring photographer, he described his signature style as "bringing back Hollywood glamor," which struck me as painfully insipid. Brendan got Spencer to introduce him around town and overnight his celebrity photos were appearing in glossy magazines. I'd known America wasn't a meritocracy but watching Brendan's effortless ascent filled my mind with fantasies of gulags and guillotines. Michael, who carried a big working class chip on his shoulder, was equally appalled. "You know why the 'invisible hand of the market' has to be invisible?" he asked. "So nobody sees it giving all the good jobs and success to well-connected rich kids."

Shortly after Brendan's arrival, Spencer asked me out to a fancy restaurant. It was a night like any other till we finished and he began toting up my share of the check. "Uh . . ." I stuttered lamely, "I think I left my wallet at home." Thereafter, at random intervals, he asked me to pay my own way. Being a penniless teenager, this led to much embarrassment. I couldn't understand why Spencer had started doing this till he let slip that Brendan thought I was a cheap hustler. "He's crazy!" I said with unfeigned outrage. True, I *had* been hustling Spencer, but only *ironically*. I actually *liked* him. Spencer let it drop, but the next time he invited me over for cocktails he suggested I bring my own vodka. Naturally, I broke up with him. The rich really are different than you and me. They're cheaper.

Soon after that came a night when I found myself without enough money for my preferred dinner of tuna and Swiss on rye with a side of potato salad. I needed to sell something for cash, but the only things of value I owned were my records and my body. Naturally, I chose the latter. Michael, who'd hustled a bit at my age, was also broke and offered to guide me through my first trick in exchange for dinner. "We'll go to the Haymarket up near the Theater District. Just remember the ground rules: Ask for the money up front. Be clear about what you will and won't do. And if the john wants you to stay more than an hour he has to pay extra." We gathered just enough change for two beers and walked thirty blocks uptown to the bar.

Inside, the Haymarket was dark, as befitted a cesspit of depravity. We bought our beers, then sat near the pool table and waited. Sat and waited. Waited and sat. The bar wasn't exactly hopping, just half a dozen middle-aged men in cheap suits leering at a dozen young guys playing pool and hanging around with wrong-side-of-the-tracks swagger. "Maybe I'm too old," I said. I'd just turned twenty and was mortally afraid of aging past attractiveness.

"Nah," said Michael.

I examined the boys more closely. Sleeveless tees revealed the taut, tanned arms of kids who played stickball in vacant lots. Deep voices boomed with cocky confidence and a total disregard for Standard English grammar. Even their un-hip feathered hair and crooked teeth oozed sexiness. "Maybe I'm too ugly."

Michael's eyebrows furrowed as if to say, "Shut up."

I only had to wait a few minutes longer before a manatee in a dark blue suit bellied up to the table nearest me and leered. "Buy you a drink?" It was on. We taxied to his apartment, attractively furnished with Japanese rice-paper screens, where we shared a joint that made me feel like an undersea creature from the briny deep. In that odd condition sexing it up with a manatee didn't seem so bad. A short while later I returned home with sandwiches, chocolate milk, and cash to spare. Victory!

I went back to the Haymarket only a half-dozen more times. The johns were mildly gross, sure, but what really bugged me was waiting to get propositioned. It often took hours, and sometimes it never happened. The other hustlers weren't friendly and there wasn't enough light to read so I'd just *sit there* going mad with boredom and self-consciousness. After one particularly annoying trick tried to stiff me on my fee, I swore off the whole business.

Michael and I weren't living *in* Manhattan so much as glimmering across its surface like sunlight on water. We lacked the roots or entanglements that would have made us real New Yorkers. I knew this well, if only instinctively, and thus it wasn't *too* hard a decision to leave town when I learned my father was dying and my mother wanted me back home. My only qualm was separating from Michael, but to my great surprise and infinite relief he decided to leave with me. It turned out that he, like me, was growing tired of the city's downsides: yucky weather, murderous traffic, surreally high rents, ubiquitous roach infestations, and—let's not forget—diseases.

Everyone said, "VD is no big deal. Just take some pills and in a week you're good as new." But I'd been infected twice (sweet, innocent little me!) and it made me feel filthy. The first time I'd gone to a city clinic where an exasperated woman demanded the names and contact information of everyone I'd slept with in the last six months. "You don't want to be spreading disease, do you? They need to come in here for testing." All I could do was shamefacedly stammer, "Uh . . . I forgot." The second time, I went to the Gay Men's Health Crisis, a new place where they didn't grill you about sex partners.

Sitting in the tiny waiting room I read the bulletin board to kill time. One notice concerned the appearance of a rare cancer in a few otherwise healthy young gay men. Normally found only among elderly males of Mediterranean descent, it manifested in purplish skin blotches. I felt a wave of terror. That very morning I'd woken up with a few purplish blotches on my legs! Ten miserable minutes later I showed them to a doctor who assured me I only had an extremely mild heat rash. I left with some pills for my other problem and forgot all about the obscure disease making its gay debut: Kaposi's sarcoma.

Chapter 6: Juan

BACK IN CALIFORNIA, MICHAEL AND I spent a rotten year watching my father die, then set about making up for lost fun. That was us teaching everyone at the house party how to dance the Shimmy Shimmy; us tripping on 'shrooms at the Frightwig concert; and us again, squabbling over nothing as we stomped through the supermarket at 3 a.m. looking for Graham crackers. To preserve energy and cash for our nightly revels we worked low-commitment jobs—Michael boxing stuff up in a warehouse, me adding numbers on a calculator in a gray cubicle—and lived rent-free in the cement-floored basement at my parents' house.

Feckless and discombobulated, yet reasonably content, we paid scant attention to reports that gay men were now contracting pneumonia along with Kaposi's sarcoma due to something called Gay Related Immune Disorder, or GRID. It seemed unfair that the disease only struck gay men, but not especially worrisome. Only a few hundred gay men out of millions had the disease, a tiny fraction of a single percent. Within a few months the "gay related" in GRID was replaced with "acquired" when the disease started popping up among Haitians, hemophiliacs, and IV drug users, an odd assortment of targets that added mystery to the menace. Still, we didn't worry. Surely, someone would develop a shot or a pill and the whole mess would be done with and forgotten like polio or Legionnaire's disease. Right?

Then I ran into an old friend from San Francisco and learned that Juan was dead. Juan would have been my first boyfriend, except I never let him call me that. We'd dated for a few months (in San Francisco before I moved to New York to be with Michael) after meeting at a house party full of guys in their twenties. I, a mere lad of nineteen, found these *older men* a bit decrepit, but also appealingly sophisticated. They drank fancy cocktails instead of the discount beer I was used to and played the stereo softly enough to allow conversation. I'd been awkwardly pretending to examine the vintage Barbie collection on the mantelpiece when a hefty young man with a shy smile came over and held out a drink of some sort. "Hi. I'm Juan. You looked thirsty." He wore pointy black boots, black peg-leg slacks, and a modishly striped dress shirt, all of which combined attractively with his floppy, straight black hair, cinnamon skin, and sultry, Mayan features. He reminded me of the guys from Question Mark & the Mysterians, a Mexican-American garage rock band from the 60s whose hit "96 Tears" I considered (and still consider) an achievement on par with Mount Rushmore, penicillin, and the moon landing. Before I knew it, Juan and I were back at his place.

Making whoopee with Juan was . . . nice, I suppose. Adequate. Acceptable. Much as I admired his style, I didn't find his body sexy. Still, any sex was way better than the absolutely none I was used to in those pre-New York days. In the morning we traded numbers and I left his apartment feeling very much a Man of The World. We went out again a few nights later and again soon after that. Somehow, without my quite noticing, we became an item. Although I wasn't really *into* Juan, I did admire his calm, patient demeanor, that he was so clearly un-rattled by the vagaries of existence. He worked as a sales clerk in a downtown department store but didn't feel discontented by his lowly station in life, probably because he'd grown up dirt poor. He seldom spoke of his early life so I only discovered this because he once made a passing reference to working as a field hand after high school. He was one of the downtrodden farmworkers on whose behalf my liberal family had boycotted grapes in the '60s. Fascinated, I demanded to know more.

"Were your parents immigrants?"

"Yup. And they took me to Mexico a few times. It was great. You could eat mangoes right off the tree and get all sticky then dive into the river to rinse off."

"Do you speak Spanish?

"It's my first language."

"Why don't you have an accent?"

"The nuns in Catholic school beat it out of me."

Despite his flawless Anglo diction, Juan was proud of his heritage and tried to educate me about Mexican culture. Diego Rivera and Pancho Villa! Salsa and serapes! Alas, I had no interest in anything that wasn't new wave and preferably from London. Racist? Let's just say ethnocentric. If my brattish indifference hurt Juan's feelings, he kept it to himself. He did harbor some ethnic resentment, though. At the time, a lot of white people were terrified of so-called "cholos": tough Mexican guys with crude tattoos, slicked-back hair, pleated pants, and pointy shoes who loitered about on street corners, presumably up to no good. Juan had no tattoos and his pleated pants made him look more like David Bowie as the Thin White Duke than a Barrio Baddie, but apparently he scared white people anyway. "When they see me and flinch I glare at them real mean and they skitter away," he said in a chipper tone that couldn't quite hide his hurt feelings. "It's hilarious."

Two or three times a week I'd join Juan at his small, tidy apartment in the Polk Gulch, the walls of which he'd decorated with picture sleeves from new wave 45s: The Suburban Lawns, Missing Persons, The Urban Verbs. We'd head out to meet Michael at The Stud or see bands, share a few beers, a few laughs, maybe dance a bit, then go back to his place and tumble into bed. A normal, healthy relationship. And yet, in Juan's presence I always heard a faint echo of Peggy Lee singing, "Is that all there is?"

After a few months of dating I'd grown restless and told Juan (oh, cruel youth, by *telephone!*) that we were through. Two weeks later he turned up on my doorstep with pleading eyes. "Can we get back together?" Juan's eyes naturally looked as if they'd been rimmed with kohl and his long lashes long reminded me of peacock's tails. Who could say no to eyes like that? I took him back. A month later, out of nothing more than sheer boredom, I dumped him for good.

And now Juan was dead. "How'd it happen?" I asked. "Was it AIDS?"

My friend shook his head. "No, no. It was something else. I'm not sure what, but *definitely* not that." It didn't seem impossible to me Juan had died from one of those rare diseases with a hard-to-remember Latin name, but I couldn't help wondering if my friend wasn't covering up the truth. A lot of people who got *sick*—a word that with the tiniest emphasis suddenly meant *dying of AIDS*—were lying about it to avoid being shunned by society. Nobody knew how the disease spread and fears were running amok. A friend told me about her out of town relatives refusing to go with her to a bar in San Francisco for fear of catching AIDS from the glasses. Michael once got sent home from his job because a co-worker felt pretty sure the tiny cold sore on his lip meant he had you-know-what. And the newspapers were full of reports about *sick* people who'd been hounded from schoolrooms, fired from jobs, or disowned by friends and family.

Of course, not everyone believed AIDS was an infectious disease. A radical Gay Libber of my acquaintance insisted AIDS was *obviously* government-sponsored germ warfare designed to wipe out undesirables. A spiritual friend conjectured that AIDS resulted from the hateful prayers of Christian fundamentalists creating a disturbance in the psychic dimension so powerful it was manifesting on the physical plane. My holistic doctor theorized gay men were expiring from the excessive use of the antibiotics used to treat sexually transmitted disease. I didn't know what to think, but for the first time in my life, a young person I'd known intimately was *gone.* Cue tiny alarm bells.

Perhaps because nobody invited me to Juan's funeral, his death never seemed totally real to me. As a result, I didn't so much mourn him as miss him the way you would a friend who's moved abroad. Now and then something would remind me of our time together and I'd feel a twinge of sadness. Mostly, though, his death left me feeling creepy, hollow, and irked with the universe.

Chapter 7: Fashion, Turn to the Left

I WATCHED WITH INCREDULITY AS MICHAEL stood before the mirror putting on first a narrow tie with horizontal stripes, then another tie of solid blue, and finally a third: forest green and covered with yellow smiley faces. "Are you really going to work like that?" I asked. Michael had recently started a job at the front desk of The Nob Hill Cinema, a dirty movie theater in San Francisco.

Michael raised his eyebrows in a manner that suggested he was a helpless pawn of fate. "My boss insists I wear a tie."

That evening I expected Michael to come home unemployed, or at least wearing a single tie. Nope!

"What did you boss say when he saw you?"

"He just laughed and shook his head."

Plenty of subcultures have an identifying "look," a fashion template full of coded significance announcing to the world here is a . . . hippie, punk, beatnik—fill in the blank. New wave was unique in that it didn't prescribe a particular look, but rather a playful attitude toward fashion. Clothes associated with middle class propriety (tasseled loafers, anything beige) or status striving (gold chains, designer jeans) were deemed un-cool, but anything else was A-OK. You could mix 'n' match handmade message tee shirts with ironic vintage-wear, iconically rebellious black leather with deliberately vulgar day-glow, or pirate gear with Native American face-paint. Genders were bent, with girls in suits and boys in make-up. Futuristic jumpsuits, wraparound sunglasses, pink and green hair, leopard-print mini-skirts? Why not?! For new wavers, life was a giant dress-up party.

Michael and I believed all this dressing up was dissidence through dandyism. By abandoning one's socially-prescribed identity in favor of expressive individualism, one opted out of the power structure. And because culture is contagious, one's opting out would encourage others to opt out—thus depriving the exploitive corporate monoculture of the docile zombie consumer-workers it needed to survive. Whether the hordes of aesthetically-mutated '80s youngsters actually contributed to the general tide of social rebellion or just diverted attention from more substantive forms of dissent (like unionizing workers or registering voters) is anyone's guess.

Michael didn't dress like a total lunatic everyday, but he frequently managed to look rather alarming. Inspired by the perversely bizarre costumes of Leigh Bowery, prominently featured in *avant-garde* fashion rags like *i-D* and *The Face*, Michael's clubbing wardrobe often wandered past new wave hip into the realms of the surreal. *Example:* he once talcum-powdered his hair white like an 18th-century aristocrat before hitting The Brig, a South of Market S&M bar. Throughout the night he'd *oh-so-casually* run his fingers through his coif, releasing a cloud of white powder onto the Leather Men. I expected this to result in our being thrown out, but the DJ and bar staff found it hilarious and the black-clad Leather Men were so bewildered they didn't know what to do.

There were plenty of straight guys into new wave, but a lot of jocks and jerks regarded dressing new wave as incontrovertible evidence of fagginess, at least for anyone not in a band. Everyone I knew got called "faggot!" so frequently it wasn't even something we bothered complaining about (and we *loved* to complain). Mostly, the hateful remarks were followed only by more hateful remarks, but sometimes they were a prelude to physical attack. Once a pack of frat brats cornered Michael on his way to a club and threatened him with a severe thrashing. He only escaped by somehow convincing them he was Billy Idol's drummer.

Now and then, Michael and I liked to dress in zany women's clothes—op art mini-dresses, paisley pantsuits, what have you—bought for cheap at thrift stores. We did this in a spirit of androgyny rather than transvestitism, never bothering with fake bosoms or trying to look like real women. Most of our drag excursions were to gay house parties where we raised no eyebrows. Once, though, Michael decided we should wear '50s prom dresses (his silver and white; mine, a dusty pink-rose) to see a bunch of hardcore bands. Hardcore was a subgenre of punk favored by guys dressed in ratty denim and flannel with studded leather accessories who enjoyed listening to screamy-angry and utterly unmelodic bands—basically punk stripped of all melody, wit, and panache. And speaking of stripped, hardcore boys were *always* going shirtless. The moment a band started playing there'd be a tangled mass of half-naked boy flesh in front of the stage. A lot of secretly gay punks got their jollies in such "mosh pits," but Michael's intent was to mock their ritualized glorification of masculinity.

As Michael and I swooshed into the On Broadway, an ancient and decrepit theater turned music venue, my body tingled with excitement. The place was jam packed with youngsters, hot, and very, very loud. Faces sneered and scowled as we pushed our way through the crowd looking for some spare space in which to stand. Despite their predilection for radical anti-authoritarian politics, hardcore boys were pretty much all gender troglodytes. Even so, we weren't being especially brave by showing up cross-dressed. Like the members of any youthful subculture, hardcore boys used clothes to carry on political conversations non-verbally, adopting or avoiding this or that symbolically-loaded fashion. Provided we didn't do anything provocative (like, say, staring at a cute guy), hardcore boys would likely react to our ball gowns not with primitive outrage, but as people challenged in debate.

Unfortunately, the club contained a danger we hadn't counted on: among the two hundred or so kids milling around were at least a couple dozen skinheads. Yikes! Meticulously outfitted with steel-toed "bovver" boots, jeans, white tee shirts, and thin suspenders, skinheads consistently managed to create some manner of violent ruckus wherever they went. And, butchest of the butch, they were not kindly disposed toward gender blurring. As panic prickled through my body like a wave of static electricity, I turned to Michael for guidance. His eyebrows wiggled slightly upwards, counseling, "Be ready to bolt, but not yet." Showing fear is never smart, so I did my best impersonation of Bette Davis from the film *Jezebel* when she brazens it out after scandalizing everyone at the a big Southern cotillion by wearing a red dress.

Before any skinheads could deliver an ass-kicking, Michael and I saw salvation in the form of Jennifer Blowdryer. Radiating the sort of Blonde Goddess sexiness that jellifies straight men's spines, she was surrounded by a small band of dudely admirers. We raced over, air-kissed, and spent the rest of the night safely ensconced in her entourage. The story wouldn't bear repeating except that one week later, Michael and I, dressed as boys, went to another hardcore show at the same venue. (Inexplicably, Michael *liked* the music.) There, to our utter confoundment, we saw two skinheads—one white and one black, though that explains nothing—*both wearing prom dresses*. What they meant by this is anyone's guess, but you couldn't have asked for better evidence that culture is contagious.

Chapter 8: Rich & Danny

THE WHITE HORSE IN NORTH OAKLAND was a swell old dive with a dark wooden interior, wobbly maroon barstools, and a scuffed linoleum floor. After a few hi-balls you could squint and see 1936—the year it opened—and the ghosts of gays gone by. Despite its attractively vintage interior, the place struck Michael and I as a bit humdrum after the vertiginous glamor of Manhattan. The music wasn't up-to-date and there was no back room for insta-sex. Still, by late 1982, we became regulars because it was the only gay watering hole within walking distance of my mom's house and life without boys and cocktails was unthinkable.

The convivial crowd at the White Horse was always up for chatting, but seldom did anyone chat me up. (For reasons unknown, my irresistibility to men had not made the trip from New York back to California.) Consequently, I was highly flattered on those rare occasions when someone bought me a drink. Usually, it was a *much* older man delusionally hoping I'd say, "Oh, thank you for this watery screwdriver, kind sir! Please allow me to offer you the use of my comely young body as a token of appreciation." Once, though, a pair of young hotties sent me a Heineken (fancy!) and beckoned me to their table.

First to speak was Rich, a garrulous, stocky fellow with curly black hair and the face of a clean-shaven satyr. He pumped me for my story and what I was all about, fitting me in his taxonomic system (*genus:* gayboy, *phylum:* new wave, *species:* wastrel). As he grilled me, Rich interrupted himself with whistles and commentary whenever cute guys entered his field of vision. "Like to get him in the sack," or, "*That* one needs to join me in my boudoir." He was an honest-to-gosh predatory wolf of the old school, the sort depicted in cartoons with a slavering tongue and eyeballs popping out of their sockets. His pal, Danny, was a lithe and classically handsome blond with a cleft chin who wore skin-tight jeans and a skimpy tee shirt so threadbare it looked to be woven of spider webs. His bedroom eyes cruised the crowd relentlessly and his languid, slouchy posture projected an ineffable lewdness. He didn't say much, but he didn't have to.

At the end of the night, Rich and Danny invited me home for a *ménage à trois*. Their house, just a few blocks away, was ordinary outside but vintage Berzerkeley within: psychedelic posters, throw pillows, surreal paintings, wind-chimes, hand-crafted candles. No sooner had I crossed the threshold than Rich and Danny dragged me to a bedroom and pounced on me like wild beasts in heat. When inflamed by passion Danny roared like a lion, which impressed me to no end. The boys knew all sorts of tricks and techniques, and before the night was done my body was electrified by sex. The next morning, I woke before my hosts. Carefully extricating myself from betwixt their bodies, I dressed and tiptoed into the hall in search of the bathroom. A naked man with straight blond hair down to his waist was walking down the hall with a mug of coffee. He pointed to a door. "The head's in there." I used the facilities and returned to find Rich yawning. "Hungry?" he asked.

While the boys and I ate cereal at the kitchen table, several nude and semi-nude men passed through to fix their own breakfasts. From snippets of conversation I gathered I'd spent the night in a commune run by Radical Faeries, a pagan sect of gay hippies devoted to erotic crafts, political activism, and Sex Magick . . . whatever *that* was. New wavers like me were supposed to disdain such Aquarian Age nonsense, but the Faeries were such throwback misfits in Reagan's new, hyper-square America that I couldn't help but find them adorable.

After that night, Rich and Danny always hung out with Michael and me at the White Horse, gossiping, gabbing, and opinionating like the shiftless barflies we were. The boys never invited me home again, but I didn't feel slighted as I could see they were busy blazing a trail of conquest through the younger set of regulars. Their sexual prowess filled me with awe and jealousy. They, in turn, found it endearingly hilarious that I was prone to mooning around in a lovelorn stupor over boys I was too shy to speak to, let alone hit on. How, in a world where almost anybody would hop into bed with almost anybody, did I manage to be so romantically inept?

One night, Rich, with a shifty look in his eye, shoved a small square of folded paper into the back pocket of my jeans. "Don't let anyone see," he whispered. Mad with curiosity, I slipped into the bathroom to discover a "Solstice Party" invitation. There was no description of what such a thing might entail, just the date, time, and address (Rich and Danny's house), all ringed by drawings of winged penises. How *distasteful*, I thought. How *vulgar*. My homosexuality revolved not around genitalia, but whole boys. I fell in love with crooked smiles, silly dances, and strange hairdos, went ape for wandering waifs and sad eyed strays with scuffy sneakers, and melted before boys who dreamed so hard they never woke up all the way. Winged penises? *Ick!*

Of course, being twenty-two and riddled with lust, I went to the party anyway. As I entered the foyer, two faerie boys asked me to disrobe, checked my clothes, then handed me a tiny cup of fruit juice laced with LSD. Feeling very "when in Rome," I downed the drink and stripped. Nude and psychedelicized, I entered the house proper and discovered it'd been done up like a seraglio with swaths of gauzy Indian fabric draped about and dim, colored lighting. Trippy music played and incense perfumed the air. Oh . . . and several hundred naked young men were cavorting with wild abandon throughout the domicile, lewdly sprawling across every floor and copulating on every piece of furniture. It was an honest-to-gosh Love-In! In the center of the room sat a giant papier-mâché statue of a golden calf, evoking the scene in Cecil B. DeMille's *Ten Commandments* when the Israelites go berserk and indulge in a wild bacchanalia.

I stood around making small talk with other recent arrivals for a while, then my mind began to jumble. First came the special effects: ultra-vivid colors, a distorted perception of space and time, an exaggerated sense of freakiness. Solid objects breathed, people became lifelike marionettes then went back to being people—stuff like that. Then my brain quit ratiocinating and I experienced the party on a purely sensate level, enjoying hour after hour of unalloyed pleasure with numerous partners. Around dawn everyone began coming down, but nobody was in any condition to travel so we all cuddled into gigantic puppy-piles and fell asleep. I woke the next morning in the certain knowledge I'd just enjoyed the best night of my life.

A few months later, in early 1983, news arrived that scientists had isolated the virus responsible for AIDS, namely HIV. HIV lived in blood and semen and thus—as many suspected—was sexually transmitted. Uh-oh. By now a couple thousand guys were sick, but I still considered that a pretty low percentage. To my dismay, though, most cases were found in New York and California, the two places I'd lived. A shadow of fear darkened my mind, but the disease had appeared so quickly it was easy to imagine it disappearing just as quickly. Some days I felt doomed, other days I felt lucky. Time would tell.

Infected or not, it was clearly no longer possible to slut around as per usual. Fortunately, someone came up with the idea of Safe Sex. This meant no anal sex without a condom, no oral sex without a condom, no fisting, no felching, no rim-ming, no sharing of sex toys. "Is mutual masturbation still OK?" asked a panicky public. "Probably," replied those in the know, "but watch out for paper-cuts or abrasions that might come in contact with ejaculate. "Is kissing safe?" asked the randy romantics. "Hmmm," said the experts, "Could be dangerous if your date recently flossed his teeth and has blood in his saliva." This was all disturbing enough, but there were a few cases of AIDS among people who claimed never to have engaged in any risky sexual behavior. Were there other modes of transmission? What if you ingested someone's perspiration? What if someone sneezed on you? What if a mosquito bit someone with AIDS and then bit you? What if, what if, what if . . . ? Plus, there were also other new diseases to worry about: herpes, hepatitis C, intestinal parasites. It began to seem as if sex would now consist of donning hazmat suits and waving through Plexiglass windows.

Some guys continued sleeping around but quit the unsafe stuff (or tried to), others turned monogamous (or tried to), a few went straight (or tried to), and a few gave up and went home. "See you when the plague's over; we're spinsters now!" A cloud of creepiness and morbidity hung over the playboy lifestyle. For a few, that held its own attractions and some guys became sluttier than ever without even a pretense of safety. Having lived so long and so deeply in the bars and bathhouses, sex had become the only means of human connection they knew. The people of light and sunshine—straights and good gays—reviled these men for their willful embrace of self-destruction, but I pitied them. In their own way they were dying for love.

Rich and Danny opted to play safe but continue bedding as many men as possible. This decision to go on regarding the world as a gigantic meat rack struck me as heroic, a bit like Londoners during the Blitz. We young men were entitled to our day in the sun, were we not? At some point I stopped seeing Rich and Danny around so much. Then someone told me Danny had died. *Poof!*—just like that. His death horrified me, but so did the thought of Rich's survival. They weren't just best friends, but inseparable like Michael and me. How would Rich function without his wingman/confidante?

A year or so after hearing about Danny, Michael and I ran into Rich at a house party. He was laughing and ogling boys as always, yet I couldn't help but see the gaping absence of Danny sitting next to him. I didn't want to ruin his good mood with condolences so I just said "Hi," and we chatted casually. A few months passed before word got around that Rich was gravely ill. Michael and I rushed to the hospital and found him in a bed looking sallow, way too thin, and covered in dark magenta lesions ranging in size from dimes to silver dollars. Wires and tubes crisscrossed his body, connecting him to mysterious, humming machines covered with lights, knobs, and switches. He looked unnaturally tired, just absolutely wrung out. How could one body even contain so much exhaustion? His eyes were open, but they stared straight ahead without moving so that it wasn't entirely clear whether he was awake.

Unsure Rich could even hear me, I forced out a mildly upbeat, "Hi," then ran out of words. Efforts at cheerfulness would surely ring hollow. He must know this would be his deathbed. Did Faeries believe in an afterlife? How do you comfort the dying? I wasn't ready for this, not by a long shot. Braver and wiser than I, Michael held Rich's hand and leaned over to whisper in his ear. I didn't hear everything he said, but it definitely included, "You don't have to stick around. It's OK to let go." After a minute Michael stood up and put his hand on my shoulder. "We're taking off now, Rich. Good-bye." I croaked out a goodbye of my own and fled into the long, beige hospital corridor so Rich wouldn't see my sad, sad face.

A few days later Rich joined Danny at that great orgy in the sky.

Chapter 9: Weimar . . . Why not?

THROUGHOUT THE MID 20TH CENTURY IT had been voguish to think of America as the New Roman Empire. Everyone knew Rome was horribly militaristic, corrupt, exploitative, and predatory, but our image of it was inextricably linked to Hollywood epics in which scantily clad hunks battled with swords and maces, nobles ate peeled grapes while servants fanned them with palm fronds, and Liz Taylor vamped around being Liz Taylor. The place was evil, sure, but also entertainingly flamboyant. And because empires sprawl across space and time, reforming them is a long-range prospect. One could scorn their injustice without being in a perpetual lather about it.

At the dawn of the '80s, a lot of people abandoned the New Rome analogy and started claiming that America was entering its Weimar phase. (Weimar, you will recall, was the short-lived period in German history prior to Hitler's ascendancy, a time beset with economic turmoil, social fragmentation, sexual decadence, and the rising tide of fascism.) Hip artists became fascinated with the era, leading to a new craze for expressionist painting, Dada-style performance, and agitprop photomontage. David Bowie covered Brecht and Weill's "Moon of Alabama" and people flocked to repertory movie houses to see Visconti's *The Damned*, Fassbinder's *Lili Marleen*, and (of course) *Cabaret*.

Parallels between 1980s America and 1920s Germany were stretched, but not totally far-fetched. The U.S. economy *was* a little shaky (unemployment passing 10 percent, homeless suddenly everywhere) and the culture *did* seem to be going schizo—simultaneously embracing a fearful, puritanical, backwards-looking religious fundamentalism (*See:* Moral Majority) and a vapid consumerism obsessed with designer labels and celebrities (*See: Interview* magazine). Decadence was everywhere in the form of cocaine-fueled hedonism, and as for fascism, President Reagan was cheerfully sponsoring a number of rightwing dictatorships and death squads in Central America.

Because Michael and I always read the newspaper at breakfast, we were usually in a state of high dudgeon by the time we finished our cereal. Along with the aforementioned crimes in Central America, Republicans were diverting cash from social programs and education to the military. Everyone (at least on our side of the political spectrum) knew this would lead to spiraling inequality, but Michael had his own corollary theory about how it would affect culture. "Without a social safety net, economic failure will be so scary everyone's going to become really cautious and careerist. Subcultures like the hippies and punks will fade away and we'll all be living in a bland, corporate monoculture . . . except for the poor, who'll become ignorant, reactionary barbarians since they won't be able to afford education."

I shared Michael's political foreboding and disgruntlement, but could never match his level of outrage—probably because my family was middle-class while his was blue-collar. Class resentment churned in Michael's gut like a nuclear reactor, powering a vitriolic hatred of all privilege and hierarchy. He was always charming strangers into revealing their financial backgrounds and then, if they came from money, steering the conversation toward the injustices visited upon the poor and the parasitical nature of unearned wealth. Only by devoting their lives and fortunes to the betterment of humanity could the affluent escape his irascible proletarian ire. Despite the intensity of his convictions, Michael was never wholly swayed by the siren song of radicalism. He mostly agreed with my personal blend of Fabian socialism and anarcho-syndicalism, but his politics were rooted on the factory floors of the Massachusetts mill town from whence he'd sprung: unions for everyone, always vote Democrat, and elect as many Kennedys as possible.

Michael's class rage also fueled a number of subsidiary peeves. The term "Emo" hadn't been coined yet, but one often ran into sensitive young men from good homes who built their identities around being ostentatiously angst-ridden. On spotting some scowling youth toting around a battered paperback copy of *Nausea,* Michael would wax sarcastic. "Oh look, another precious pretty boy dabbling in existential misery. Funny how the morbidly obese lady driving that bus or that old Black shoeshine man can be cheerful, but that perfectly healthy guy attending school on his father's dime is just too sensitive to manage a smile." Such complaints became so frequent Michael could eventually spit out *"existentialmiseryprettyboy"* as if it were a single syllable.

Despite his extreme partisanship, Michael was still a dedicated contrarian. In any group moving toward consensus his whole body would twitch as if bedeviled by crawling bugs. After a minute of holding it in, he'd invariably blurt out some opinion guaranteed to annoy and outrage everyone present. (*Example:* In a room full of people discussing the necessity of violent revolution he might suddenly insist that royalty sets a good example of poise and politesse for the commoners.) He despised groupthink and believed that true statements, when recited with sufficient condescension or sanctimony, become lies, their factual accuracy obliviated by their hidden agenda of self-congratulation.

Michael's contrarianism also manifested in a fondness for antagonistic character dissection. This invariably began with an ominous, "The trouble with *you* is . . . " He tried to maintain a cold detachment when "reading someone to filth," but sometimes he worked himself into such a tizzy all semblance of civility fell away. During one dressing-down he deliberately spit a bit of brownie into a friend's face. "You," he said with withering contempt, "are a common, *common* queen." Amazingly, the victim of the brownie assault forgave Michael within hours, telling me later, "It was that second 'common' that really got to me. I figured he was right."

Positive reactions to Michael's harangues were not unusual. Sure, many of his targets fled or expelled him from their homes, but often some miraculous transformation of character took place instead. Overcautious boys dyed their hair blue, girls dumped their sexist boyfriends, and people who'd only been idly thinking about finding a hobby ran out and bought guitars or picked up paintbrushes. What made him so magically persuasive confounded me at first, but eventually I realized that people—even dullards—could see his criticism came from caring. Michael's Catholic childhood had left its mark. He didn't just want to change his target-victims' behavior. He wanted to save their souls.

According to Michael, the trouble with *me* was that I didn't appreciate how lucky I was. "You grew up in a big house with parents who read books and took you to art museums and served whole grain bread!" I'd always felt like one of life's unfortunates because I'd been bullied for being gay, but seeing my childhood through his eyes, I realized I *was* lucky. This admission was made easier because Michael, despite his hardscrabble background, also felt lucky. Simple pleasures like barbershop haircuts, ice cream cones, or sunny days in the park made him euphoric. This capacity for easy delight was, I suspect, one source of his anger. He felt the low-level discontent so many people live with insulted the miracle of existence and deserved pitiless reprimanding. I disliked acknowledging my good fortune and cherished my discontent, but eventually Michael bullied me into an attitude of gratitude that (much to my chagrin) made me a happier person.

Another of my troubles, according to Michael, was snobbery. Once I snickered at a fellow's mullet: a short-in-front/long-in-back hairstyle that new wavers considered grotesquely uncool. On hearing me, Michael's eyebrows knit into an avenging scowl. "Maybe that guy works sixty hours a week on an assembly line and doesn't have time to read imported magazines telling him how the hip kids in London are wearing their hair this week. Or maybe his parents are religious nuts and his rock 'n' roll rebel mullet is a big step toward freedom for him."

I parried with a hastily concocted theory. "Humans are innately inclined to hierarchy and low-caste members invariably ape high-caste members. Isn't it better if the high caste sets barriers around its status based on good taste instead of wealth or illustrious ancestry?"

Michael returned the serve. "First, social hierarchy is only an innate *tendency*, not an unavoidable condition. Second, what's considered good taste is subjective. The mullet is 'business in the front, party in the back' signifying the wearer *has to* accommodate the working world, but *desires* the freedom to party, a conflict you'd be more aware of if you weren't a spoiled rich kid." Calling me a rich kid bordered on the absurd as I seldom had two nickels to rub together, but I conceded Michael was right about mullets. Since childhood I'd seen life from an outsider's point of view. Michael taught me to see it from the underdog's as well.

Alas, my confessing to the crimes of being lucky and a snob did nothing to abate Michael's one-man class war. He flaunted his humble background in every debate, implying it gave him both greater social insight and moral superiority. In defense, I did a bit of *reductio ad absurdum* jiu-jitsu by comically exaggerating my own privilege, imitating the dated, supercilious speech patterns of upper-crust Brits I'd seen on a thousand *Masterpiece Theater* costume dramas. Like the musical voice and fey mannerisms I'd acquired when embracing my homosexuality, this affectation somehow locked in—becoming an inalterable part of my persona.

Michael and I each had other friends, but they always remained provisional since Michael continually scrutinized everyone for moral and political shortcomings. He was always bringing people up on charges of smoking too much pot, not caring enough about the plight of the downtrodden, being social climber-y, New Age-y, tediously predictable, old-fashioned, insufficiently appreciative of David Bowie, persnickety, or . . . almost anything really. During deliberations Michael usually played prosecutor, and I, the bleeding heart defense attorney. Despite my best efforts to make excuses and find loopholes, he pronounced most everyone guilty. Sentences came from his eyebrows, which lowered with the finality of a gavel as he solemnly pronounced the person in question to be a jerk, cad, creep, or cretin. I'd sadly agree, and thank my lucky stars I had a good friend who could see through everybody, even me.

As the '80s wore on, AIDS took the place of the Holocaust in our Weimar worldview. Since there was no cure on the horizon, prevention became our only hope: end HIV transmission and eventually the plague will end. *Salvation through Safe Sex!* Using a condom was patriotic (*gay*triotic?) and carried moral weight, like fighting with the French Resistance. Everyone knew sex with condoms was something like 88 percent less fun, but we *always* used them. It's amazing how vigilant one can become, even in the throes of passion, with the Angel of Death hovering over one's shoulder.

Chapter 10: Toaster

"IT'S FAST MONEY," SAID NICK, A cocky 24-year-old barfly with short black hair and a sexy uni-brow. "And it's not dangerous like people think." I could barely hear. The Stud was always noisy and he was speaking in the hushed voice suitable for matters of subterfuge and intrigue. "Nobody's gonna dismember you and leave your body parts in trash bags all over town or anything. You just make a lot of lonely old guys happy. I work, like, two, three nights a week and I'm always flush." The promise of short hours intrigued me even more than the money. My job selling popcorn and candy behind the counter at the Strand Theater swallowed too many hours I'd prefer to spend drinking cocktails and reading movie star bios.

"How do you meet your clients?"

"You run an escort ad. Just costs a few bucks a week. After a while you get repeat customers and you don't even need that."

"You really think anyone would want me?"

Nick dismissed this fear with a wave of his hand and a noise that sounded like *"Ffwoou."*

"What about my hair?" I was sporting a short Mohawk, a punk hairdo that was not quite yet mainstream.

Nick thought for a moment. "Well, you'd be a specialty item. But that's *good*. Gets you a readymade niche market." He gave me an appraising look, his massive brow furrowing. "I just hate to see a kid like you going to waste."

Over the next few weeks I pondered becoming a Call Boy. Michael and I had moved out of my mom's basement and were sharing a one-bedroom in S.F.'s Polk Gulch, so I could definitely use the extra money. And there'd be no sitting around a bar waiting like there was at the Haymarket. Sure, some Call Boys probably *were* dismembered now and again (or else why would Nick have brought it up?), but people working behind counters got shot in hold-ups. And wasn't serving popcorn starting to feel like a Living Death anyway, the endless repetition of butter and boredom slowly crushing my spirit?

Figuring what the heck, I took out an ad in the back of the *Bay Area Reporter* stating my age, physical dimensions, and proclivities under the billing "Punk Hunk" and waited. As soon as the issue hit the streets my phone began to ring.

My first client was a doughy middle-aged businessman with a comb-over. The sex was unpleasant, but it only lasted twenty minutes and paid as much as three nights at the popcorn stand. My second was a shoe-fetishist specializing in Converse All-Stars who'd rigged up a complicated system of pulleys and mirrors in his garage. Fascinating! The third was a doddering Englishman in a three-piece suit who was so ancient all he could do sexually was just sort of marvel at me, which was perfect. Most johns, unfortunately, wanted actual sex, which was perfectly awful.

After a few weeks, I got a repeat customer: a generic ruddy-faced, silver-haired businessman in his late fifties, Clarence. After our third tryst, Clarence asked me if I'd help serve at a party for his oldest and dearest friends. Same pay but no sex. All I had to do was pass around hors d'oeuvres. The proposal made me leery (would the party turn Satanic, dismember me and leave my body parts around town in trash bags?), but I said yes because I always say yes to everything.

I arrived slightly late at Clarence's blandly furnished apartment in Twin Peaks (aka "The Swish Alps") and found it full of men in business suits. Not having asked what to wear I dressed in jeans and a tight tee shirt. Clarence didn't seem to mind and set me to work passing around pigs-in-blankets and Ritz cracker canapés. The men were discussing business, sports, blockbuster movies, and cars. What exquisite tedium! I'd never encountered gay men so utterly bereft of sparkle. Sure, they'd all come of age back when homosexuals needed discretion to survive, but this was 1983 for cryin' out loud. Couldn't they all just loosen up? Toward the end of the night I got my wish when a pair of squiffy fellows got into a spat that concluded with the following exchange:

"Oh, what do you know, *Karen*?"

"More than you, *Verna*!"

Clarence, face flushed like an Easter ham, pointed at me and hissed to his friends, "I don't think our young man here needs to know about our *girl* names."

So, the party guests weren't as boring as they pretended! Learning the men hid feminine alter egos made me like them more, but also made me sad. In donning mannish facades, I felt they'd squelched the creativity and self-expression that could have made them interesting.

I'd been in *the life* for a couple of months when I found myself in the studio apartment of a john I'll call "John." As was customary, I asked for my fee up front upon arriving. John, slender, hairy, beady eyed, and pale as a white crayon, was already stripping out of his clothes. "I ran out of cash but my friend's coming by with some money he owes me. He'll be here any minute. Let's get started."

"No," I said. "Let's wait."

John sat his tiny, nude body down on his lumpy brown sofa. "He won't be long. Have a seat. You know, I'm sure you have stuff to do later. Why don't we just get started so we can finish up quickly and you can do your stuff?"

I sat gingerly on the opposite end of the sofa. "Thanks, but I'll wait." I knew I should've left right then, but after a decent first month (everyone wanted to sample new boys), business had slowed *way* down. Plus, I needed the money. My toaster had recently developed the bad habit of setting bread on fire. Toast was the centerpiece of my culinary repertoire and I needed a new one.

"I swear, my friend's on the way. Why would I lie? Do I look like a liar? Let's just get started."

I folded my arms petulantly. "I'll believe you have a friend coming over when I see him."

"Soon," said John. He looked and sounded utterly sincere, and probably could've passed a polygraph test.

"I'll wait fifteen minutes," I said.

John smiled. "You won't even have to wait that long. He'll be right here. Really, we might just as well get started."

Obviously, this dreadful scene had played out before. The "just get started" mantra sounded like the tried and true ploy of a serial cheapskate. After a quarter hour of sitting peevishly on the sofa I stood and barked, "OK, *John*, you have totally *wasted* my evening and *I'm leaving.*"

John turned frantic. "Noooooo! He's *coming!*"

I'd been ready to leave empty-handed but this brazenness infuriated me. "And I *demand* compensation for my wasted time in the form of . . ." I looked around. John's apartment was downscale. No espresso machine. No fine china. Just a lot of mismatched furniture, but in the kitchenette . . . "Your toaster!" Indignant and adrenalized, I marched over to the appliance and pulled the plug.

"Don't take that toaster," whined John. He slithered into the kitchenette and knelt before a cupboard. My blood froze. Was there a gun in there? "Take *this* one." He stood up holding a second toaster. I was floored. Who owns two toasters?

"How do I know that toaster works?" I asked suspiciously.

"Test it," said John, with an unctuous grin. He wasn't scared of me, or even embarrassed, but he wouldn't deny me my booby prize.

I tried to sound icy and commanding. "Bread please."

John retrieved a slice from the fridge and handed it to me. I plugged in the second toaster and popped it in.

"My friend *is* coming," said John. Still hopeful. Still naked.

I didn't say anything, just glared. While waiting for the toast, my rage turned to humiliation. This was not the glamorous career of my imaginings. This was sordid and annoying. I decided to quit hustling. I was a *bad* hustler.

"Seems OK," I allowed, when the bread came up golden brown. I unplugged the toaster and looked at the door. I'd never stolen anything before. Heck, I was such a goody two-shoes I never even littered! Was it really moral to go through with this? Yes, I decided, most definitely, yes. I was teaching John a valuable lesson about honesty, good manners, and not wasting hustlers' time. I tried to pick up my toaster but the sides were still hot. Wishing John weren't watching me with his beady, and inexplicably still hopeful eyes, I took off my jacket and wrapped it around the toaster. Then, mustering what little dignity I could, I stalked out of the apartment.

Chapter 11: Nightmare in Hell House

BY 1984, AIDS DEATHS WERE SKYROCKETING and epide-
miologists speculated that *over half* of all sexually active gay
men were infected. I figured, given my history, that the
chances of my being lucky lay somewhere between zilch and
nada. Five years was the outside length of time from infection
to the outbreak of "full-blown AIDS," with death invariably
following within a year or two. The inescapable conclusion: I
would die within seven years. The prospect of an early grave
left me feeling cheated and miserably depressed, sure, but
also a little relieved. There was no need to chose a career or
save for a rainy day. No need to grow up and be responsible.
The only sensible course of action would be to cram as much
merriment as humanly possible into my few remaining years. I
might die young, but I'd go out swinging!

In this slightly desperate, slightly despondent frame of
mind I met and became enraptured with a strange and nefar-
ious young man I'll call Hank. Hank dressed like a cross
between a So-Cal skate rat, a member of the Velvet
Underground, and a depression-era Okie farmer—a style that

perfectly flattered his longish dirty blond hair, sinewy body, and goofily handsome face. The very sight of him turned me into a panting, sex-crazed imbecile. Miraculously, Hank liked me too. He held my hand in public (still potentially lethal thanks to anti-gay vigilantes), met me at the door with a kiss, traced hearts on my arm with his finger, and once even spontaneously stuck a flower in my hair. He made me feel pretty.

Ours could have been a fairy tale romance but for one teensy problem . . . Hank shot speed and would reach for a needle with no more thought than you or I might reach for a salad fork. I enjoyed all sorts of pills and powders while nightclubbing, but this horrified me. I believed syringes to be both passé *and* déclassé, plus I suffered from a nervous dread of sharp objects. Hank understood my aversion and agreed never to "bang" in my presence. I decided this would be an acceptable compromise because . . . well, he was sexy and I'd be dead soon anyway.

A cheerful extrovert, Hank worked at a pizzeria where he was always making new friends to drag home for impromptu kitchen parties. These were jolly affairs fueled by cheap beer, gossip, flirtation, and tiny "bumps" that kept everyone motor-mouthing well into the dawn. Michael joined me at Hank's regularly, entertaining everyone with his arch and quasi-facetious opinionizing. He had his doubts about Hank, suspecting him of being an insubstantial Good Time Charlie, but they eventually bonded over their mutual distaste for the new gay trend toward aspirational upscale conformity.

In a nutshell: lots of gay guys, spooked by AIDS and resurgent homophobia, were trying to achieve respectability through conspicuous consumption. Designer label clothing replaced the '70s-style he-man duds and the Castro was awash in men dressed as if for a guest appearance on *Dynasty*, the insanely popular prime-time soap opera about oil-rich jerks.

This wasn't an entirely new phenomenon. For decades downtown department stores had been one of the few places that hired obviously gay men and many obviously gay men, out of gratitude and/or survival instinct, became aficionados of the shopping lifestyle. Hank loved to rail against such "piss elegance" and even spray-painted "Queers Against Gays" on a wall South of Market—shocking as this was years before the word "queer" got re-appropriated by progressive politicos.

Hank and I had been dating a few weeks when a pair of rooms opened up at his flat in the seedy, crime-ridden Lower Haight. I loved living with Michael in the Polk Gulch, one of the few S.F. neighborhoods with enough tall buildings to feel truly urban, but to my mind, cohabiting with a lover spelled lots of s-e-x. At first, Michael didn't want to come with me, pointing out that Hank was an irresponsible reprobate, but he caved on learning we'd each have our own room for $120 a month—insanely cheap, even for then.

Hank's flat, nicknamed "Hell House," occupied the bottom floor of a ramshackle Victorian. The house's gingerbread exterior had faded to a color only describable as weather-beaten and its tiny front yard was a botanical necropolis, but the real disaster area was inside. Leprous walls shed paint and plaster, leaky plumbing irrigated micro-jungles of mold and mildew, and the whole place tilted alarmingly to one side, a vivid reminder that in San Francisco the ground beneath one's feet is apt to shift whimsically. The phone number there (we all shared a single line) was UNDEAD 7, perfect because there were seven roommates. We all held jobs but devoted the bulk of our energies (which were prodigious, thanks to Hank's abundant supply of amphetamines and generous nature) to a never-ending debauch. In the louche chaos of Hell House people watched *The Jetsons* on 'shrooms, created sculptures out of old telephones, performed Satanic bondage rituals, experimented with fabric dyes, dolled up in drag, feuded, debated, and danced the Watusi.

Shortly after moving in I discovered why our rent was so low: the landlord was an old perv who insisted we deliver the rent to him in person then answered the door without any pants on. He'd originally rented the space to Critter, the prettiest boy alive. Straight men cruised Critter right in front of their wives, traffic on busy streets ground to a halt when he skateboarded by, and legions of admirers showered him with food, drugs, money, and lodging, getting nothing in return but the whisper of a smile. By the time I moved in some rich girl had spirited Critter away to her mansion, but he occasionally came back to visit. Seeing the way Hank leered at him, the way *everybody* leered at him, made me crazy jealous. How pleasant it would be to float above life's obstacles on a violet cloud of adoration!

Hank was mad for mid-century modernist design and continually scavenged thrift-stores for Sascha Brastoff ceramics, Vera scarves, and Eames-y looking chairs. Alas, drug mania made him somewhat indiscriminate, and, along with a few real treasures, he dragged home mediocre table lamps, malfunctioning appliances, broken toys, scratchy records, amateur oil paintings, and, oh, just anything that wasn't nailed down. Tsunamis of junk flooded from his room into the hallway and kitchen, eliciting complaints which were invariably met with sincere apologies and frantic clean ups. The neatness never lasted long though as Hank was always absentmindedly disorganizing things with abandoned searches and improbable art projects.

Hank also scavenged people. His best find was an achingly sincere blonde girl with high cheekbones and expensive clothes who claimed to have written a hit song for Pat Benatar. She'd drop by to say hello, buy drugs from Hank, do them, spend a few days going from room to room socializing, and then when she started to lose steam say, "Oh, I think I'm coming down with the flu." We'd all laugh and say, "No Genevieve, you're *crashing*!" but she'd shake her pretty head and insist it was the flu, then curl up on someone's bed for three days until she felt well enough to either buy more drugs or leave.

One day I came home from work to hear that the police had picked up Hank on a charge of possession. This shocked me. *All sorts* of people did *all sorts* of drugs *all the time* but nobody ever got arrested. However had he managed it? I asked around, but nobody seemed to know. The next day I tromped down to San Francsico's gigantic gray Hall of Justice for visiting hours. There I found Hank standing behind a thick, scratchy Plexiglass window wearing an orange jumpsuit and a sheepish half-smile, as if getting caught embarrassed him. Feeling like some mousy wife in an old crime drama I put my face up to the metal screen for speaking with inmates and asked if he was OK. He told me he was in the queen tank so he wasn't getting raped or beaten and I shouldn't worry. He seemed more concerned about my anxiety than his own predicament. I went home slightly reassured but couldn't really relax until two days later when the cops released him and dropped the charges.

Cohabiting did not, as I'd hoped, lead to lots of s-e-x. In fact, night after night, Hank left me sleeping alone while he did speed. I tried joining his narcotic frenzies but failed due to my innate predilection for slothfulness. The rare occasions we slept together resulted in spectacular bouts of whoopee, but by rare I mean *rare*. Though terrified of losing him, I began nagging Hank to quit. He ignored me until one night I threw a world-class hissy fit, replete with shrill accusations, histrionic arm flinging, tearful entreaties, and angry wailing. Hank agreed to go clean and for three weeks he kept his word, just swilling forty-ouncers and taking lots of naps. The apartment got a thorough tidying and Hank once again slept in my bed. Then—*boom!*—he went back to his old ways. I asked why, and he said because when he shot up he could "see God." Being an agnostic, this meant nothing to me. I wanted to break up but also didn't, so I compromised by staying with him but sleazing around on the side.

When he relapsed, Hank went really berserk. He lost his pizzeria job (stealing?) and started working at an erotic bakery. Our refrigerator was always filled with leftover cakes shaped like penises and breasts. He also began hanging out with scary weirdoes, including a fellow whose picture had recently appeared in the paper for biting a policeman and a skinny skinhead named Stove who was dating a chubby girl who dressed like a gothic Stevie Nicks and claimed to be a witch. Most distressingly, Hank accidentally left his "works" in the kitchen sink a couple of times, the sight of which seriously creeped me out. Six months ago, any one of these transgressions (except maybe the cakes, I love cakes) would've sent me running for the hills, but—boiled frog syndrome in action—I'd slowly grown accustomed to lunacy.

As the most responsible person in Hell House (Virgo, Virgo rising), the utilities wound up in my name. Well, maybe not so much responsible as gullible. Every month I had to hound all these crazy, drugged-out people for money and it got harder and harder. Finally, I complained to Hank, "We owe four hundred dollars and everybody's broke and the house is a mess and you don't make me feel pretty any more. I'm leaving!" I stomped off to my room but before I could slam the door, Hank grabbed me by the hand. I tried to pull away but he kissed me ever so sweetly and coaxed me back to the kitchen with a line. I snorted away my anger and decided to give him one last chance.

A few days later, I came home from work cranky and tired to find the kitchen, which I'd recently cleaned, under a sea of rubbish: macramé plant holders, deflated inflatable wading pools, dented car parts, dirty stuffed animals, I don't remember what all—use your imagination and go wild. In the middle of the maelstrom sat Hank, busily disassembling the toaster. Surrounding him was a motley horde of lowlifes finishing off the last of a lasagna I'd made from scratch (and hadn't even tasted yet as I'd been letting it sit overnight so the flavors could marry). Infuriated, I did what any sensible sitcom wife would do, stomped my foot and shrieked, "I'm going home to mother!" Seeing my implacable rage, Hank didn't even try to stop me.

Within days Michael and I were back in my mom's basement. This time, it seemed heavenly. No lunatics! No mess!

Alas, I missed Hank terribly. We'd lived together less than six months; maybe I hadn't given him enough of a chance. After all, nobody's perfect, and anyone who was would probably be really annoying. A few weeks slogged by, each lonelier than the last, then Hank called. His voice produced a Pavlovian response: my heart salivated.

We'd just begun to trade pleasantries when Hank cut to the chase. On leaving I'd taken my name off the utilities and Hell House no longer had electricity. Nobody living there had money or credit and they couldn't convince PG&E to turned it back on. Would I reopen my account? Pretty please? He cared about me! He still wanted to be my boyfriend! It was winter and they couldn't use their space heaters! He loved me! This gusher of smarm so appalled me I couldn't speak. Confronted by my frosty silence, Hank began laughing. He knew his pitch was falling on deaf ears. Lesser addicts would have gotten angry, but he just wished me well and hung up.

Given that Hank was gay *and* an IV drug user, his demise from AIDS seemed inevitable. A couple of friends kept in touch with him, so I knew I'd hear right away when he got *sick*. Years went by . . . nothing. Eventually I heard he'd made the switch from speed to beer, married some guy, and moved to a small town back east where he remained, thankfully, undead.

Chapter 12: AIDS, AIDS, and More AIDS

BACK AT MY MOM'S PLACE IN the suburbs, the terror I'd been living with for the last couple of years faded to a mild, if persistent, anxiety. The magical thinking part of my brain (the part that believed you could escape the boogeyman by hiding under blankets) believed AIDS preferred to snatch its victims from the streets of urban gay ghettoes rather than tree-lined suburban lanes. Remarkably, I retained this calm frame of mind even after starting my new job: conducting surveys for the AIDS Foundation.

Every night, from 5 to 9, I sat in a gray office cubicle and phoned random households looking for people in high-risk categories (mostly gay guys) to enquire about their sex lives. The goal was to see how much the public knew about AIDS and gauge the effectiveness of various Safe Sex campaigns. A lot of people were understandably shy about divulging intimate details to a stranger over the phone, but I overcame their reservations by sounding bored, enunciating terms like "intravenous drug use" and "anal sex" so they came out sounding dull as "variable annuity life insurance" or "automatic transmission."

Risky sex was way down, but not everyone managed to stay a hundred percent safe. Someone would tell me about a little slip and I'd think, "That could cost you your life."

Interviewing the infected was always awkward. They tried to respond to my questions in the same calm professional demeanor I used, but their voices were invariably tinged with sadness and/or terror. Only once did I run across someone with a different reaction. "The politicians just *don't care*," said the disembodied voice, breaking with anger. "If AIDS affected straight people, they'd be *doing* something, but they're *glad* to see us die. We're just *faggots*." He went on this way for a good five minutes, then apologized for his outburst and finished the interview. I thought to myself, *He's right, but what're you gonna do?*

I was working nights because I'd enrolled at UC Berkeley. It'd been three long, decadent years since I dropped out of SF State, and replacing drugs, drag, hustling, and nightclubs with textbooks and term papers felt delightfully wholesome. I was, however, determined to gay up the university at bit, so I designed an AIDS survey for use in one of my sociology classes. Most of the students took it without comment, but a good half-dozen squealed, *"Eeew!"* or laughed nervously when I put the survey on their desk. One student refused to touch it until I shamed him. "You can't catch AIDS from a sheet of paper with the word 'AIDS' on it." The news was full of similar paranoia—policemen wearing rubber gloves to arrest gays, dentists refusing to treat AIDS patients, politicians advocating quarantine, and teenage Ryan White getting driven out of school by a mob of "concerned" parents.

One couldn't help but worry things would get worse, given plague's history of inciting bizarre and violent behavior. During the Middle Ages, as the Black Death approached Sweden, King Magnus ordered his subjects to go barefoot on Sundays to appease the divine wrath everyone blamed for the pestilence, and a German prophylactic measure involved stuffing Jews into wine barrels and tossing them into the Rhine. It was unlikely gays would be charged with poisoning wells using concoctions derived from lizards, snakes, and spiders (as had the Jews), but a few figures on the Religious Right were claiming that homosexual sex actually produced the AIDS virus. Scary!

I didn't enjoy thinking about AIDS all the time, but the world kept reminding me. I was in the weight room at the gym when a guy in his late twenties turned to his workout buddy: "Hey, what does 'GAY' stand for? 'Got AIDS yet?' *Hyuck, hyuck, hyuck.*" I wanted to upbraid the joker, but what could I say? Were I to challenge his insensitivity he *might* refrain from making AIDS jokes in the future, but that wouldn't make him any less glad to see my demise. Anyway, I didn't want bigots to censor their speech in public; I wanted them to stop hating gay people. The only way to effect that change would be to maintain a high quotient of likability. Also, the guy hadn't been speaking to me, so admonishing him would be tantamount to an admission of eavesdropping. I decided to keep my trap shut, which left me a little seethe-y.

Michael was less restrained. We were in Rasputin Records once when the store began playing some bratty punk song with homophobic lyrics. Michael marched up to the counter and demanded it be taken off. "Oh, lighten up," suggested the hip, rocker chick behind the counter.

Michael smiled coldly. "Would you *lighten up* if the song were making fun of girls with hideously disfiguring acne?"

The counter girl's face paled, then reddened, then she screamed loudly enough that everyone in the store looked our way. "Out! Out now!" She and another clerk ran over, grabbed our arms, and hustled us out the door. She was hollering and I was hollering and Michael was hollering and the other clerk was hollering and I had no idea what any of us was saying. Standing on the street, surrounded by people who never got thrown out of anywhere, I felt a wave of stomach-churning shame at being party to Michael's unkindness. The counter girl *did* have hideous acne. Having had terrible acne as a teen I well knew the loneliness and misery it could bring.

I turned to Michael. "Two wrongs don't make a right!"

Michael harrumphed. "If she can't take it, she shouldn't dish it out."

"But you're not going to make her like gay people by *insulting* her."

"I don't care if she likes gay people. I just wanted her to take that stupid song off. If gay people raised a stink every time a straight person did something homophobic maybe they'd quit being so bigot-y."

"They might quit *acting* bigot-y in public, but they wouldn't quit *thinking* bigot-y thoughts in private. I'm not saying we should ignore bigotry, but militancy isn't *always* the most effective strategy for confronting it."

"At least the employees in that one store will have to think twice before acting like homophobia is socially acceptable. They'll understand being bigot-y has consequences."

I could see bigot-y was going to be our new favorite word of the week. "I wouldn't be surprised if that scene made the people in that store *more* bigot-y than they already were. It's human nature that people don't like to be embarrassed or admit they're wrong."

"So, you want to eradicate homophobia with what . . . charm? That is so naïve!"

"And you want to eradicate homophobia by making straight people scared of our raising a fuss? They *like* beating gay people to a pulp. They *enjoy* it."

Michael shook his head. "A small minority of sadists enjoy it, but eventually the general public will turn against images of sustained brutality."

"You're counting on the general public's better nature and you say *I'm* naïve?"

Michael's eyebrows glowered remorselessly. "That girl had it coming."

Michael always projected surety and self-confidence, but something in his eyes hinted at a subterranean lake of psychic pain. Being gay had never caused *me* any psychic pain, but I'd grown up Bay Area-style, with sex education in the schools and pro-gay propaganda like *Tales of the City* serialized in the morning *Chronicle*. Michael had been raised to believe in a just and merciful God who planned to burn him eternally in a lake of fire for his "disordered passions." Maybe he was more fragile than I'd thought. Casting moral scrupulosity to the wind, I dropped the subject.

* * *

IN THE EVENINGS, MICHAEL AND I became, once again, White Horse regulars. Over the course of a couple years I managed to date Kenny, who vaguely resembled Matthew Broderick from *Ferris Beuller's Day Off*; Olaf, who reminded me of Nicholas Cage from *Valley Girl*; and Jared, who—if you squinted hard—looked like Anthony Michael Hall in *The Breakfast Club*. All of them, alas, slipped through my fingers—possibly because I was not a Great Lover. I had trouble losing myself in The Act since it involved the release of substances every bit as frightening as plutonium 238 or hydrochloric acid.

My mother (now comfortable enough with gays to rent a room in our house to a guy dating a Catholic priest) noticed my romantic pining. Though she'd never before offered romantic advice, she took me aside and quietly said, "I know it's hard when you're young, but try not to just run after the good-lookers." I thanked her for her concern, but it was no use. I'd gone boycrazy. I wanted to play with *boys*, dance with *boys*, study *boys*, possess *boys* and be possessed by *boys*. I *worshipped boys* even as I resented them for enslaving me. *Boys* haunted me as I hunted them. *Boys* were a vibration that quivered my flesh, an aroma that unsettled my soul. I was forever rubbing my eyes in bedazzlement, gasping for breath, and going crazy-out-of-my-head-nutso because of *boys! Boys! BOYS!*

But . . . every time I thought of *boys* (about once every forty-seven seconds), a tiny voice in the back of my head whispered, "AIDS."

Chapter 13: The Popstitutes: 1986

ONE NIGHT WHILE LOAFING AROUND THE White Horse, Michael and I got to discussing the wretched state of Gay Lib. Everywhere anti-discrimination laws were Dead On Arrival, a proposition calling for the quarantine of people with HIV was on California's November ballot, and—more troubling yet— I'd been queer-bashed. It had happened a few nights before when I'd left the bar alone shortly after midnight. A pack of teens, I couldn't see how many, appeared from nowhere and sprinted down the otherwise deserted street in my direction. Mind blank with terror, I ducked around the corner and ran like mad. After a brief chase, I found myself cornered in the doorway of an abandoned gas station thinking *I'm dead! I'm dead! I'm dead!* As the teens closed in, I crumpled my body into a defensive ball and said my (completely agnostic) prayers. One after another, the teens took turns jumping up and down on my back as if I were a trampoline. Then they vanished quick as they'd come. No blood or broken bones, but scary as heck. I told everyone all about it at the bar the next night, but such occurrences were so common my fellow barflies barely offered a minute's sympathy. "Oh Mary, I'm sorry but we all get our gay knocks sooner or later."

Michael and I found such resignation ranklesome. Lesbians were continually outraged by patriarchy, pollution, war, poverty, racism, cars, meat, capitalism, ableism, looksism, speciesism— you name it. Why were gay men so apathetic? We'd dabbled with envelope stuffing, campaign phone banking, and rally attending, but such socially-sanctioned activism felt tepid. After some careful, if sodden, consideration we hit upon a perfect plan to rouse and rally our fellow deviants: We'd form a band! Not just another musical group, but an agitprop spectacle advocating political engagement, DIY creativity, fabulous fashions, gender anarchy, and Safe Sex. We'd become celebrated culture heroes, showered with fame, money, critical respect, and (*please, please, please*) groupies. It sounded like the best idea ever until I remembered something.

"But Michael, we don't play any instruments."

Michael's eyebrows raised scoffingly. "Don't be silly. This is the '80s. There are *machines* to play the instruments *for* us."

The next day Michael ran out and bought a small, white plastic Casio keyboard from a toy store. Not only could it simulate dozens of instruments, it contained a tape recorder that turned two second sound bites into notes one could play on the keyboard. *Totally* Space Age. Over the next few weeks he used that and a four-track recorder to create a series of tape loops that would provide our band's sonic foundation. When he'd finished, his face shone with pride. "Listen!" He pressed a button.

Ka-chung, ka-chung, ka-chung, screeek! Chung, chung, chung, screeek!

Now, I like experimental art bands as much as the next guy, but I hadn't wanted us to *be* one. I wanted us to be a radio-friendly, danceable new wave pop sensation. How else could our message reach the masses? The masses were on the dance floor! The masses were listening to the radio! In the best of all possible worlds, we'd produce a stirring gay pop anthem like Bronski Beat's "Why?" (To this day, that song's initial synth-wash floods my mind with hope and resolve.) Michael may have loved debating the issues of the day, but when it came to his personal artistic output he brooked no criticism, so I kept my reservations to myself. "Sounds great!"

Music taken care of, Michael turned his attention to lyrics, forever working on a series of songs penned onto yellow legal pads kept in a worn leather briefcase. He let me help with a line here, a rhyme there, but only solicited my input when completely stuck. His compositions included "Mortals Possessed," which mocked the preciosity of angst, "The Mugging," which described a queer bashing, "Cursed with Good Taste," which bemoaned the bourgeois aesthetic of subtlety, and "Camp is Dead," which questioned the potential of irony to subvert the dominant cultural paradigm: *"Camp's dead, bumped its head. Like Karen Carpenter, a barren art theater."* Except to plug condoms, his lyrics never addressed AIDS or mortality. I suspect this was from pure hopelessness. When the sky is falling, why run around saying the sky is falling? It's not like anyone can dodge the whole sky.

Our bar buddy Brad was in on the deal. Brad looked rather like the young Brian Eno, studied fine art at Berkeley, and played the piano, accordion, *and* saxophone. Best of all, he

had this amazing giggle, a giggle of such playfulness, inno-
cence, and whimsy it could clear a room of bad vibes in
seconds. With Brad and Michael taking care of the music, all
I had to do was dance around, sing back-up, and occasionally
push a button on the Casio.

We called ourselves The Popstitutes, which was supposed to
suggest Pop Prostitutes, a reference to one of our convoluted
critical theories about the injustice of people selling themselves as commodities . . . or something like that, I forget
exactly. Naturally we all had to wear *really* spectacular outfits.
I taped translucent red and blue shopping bags into a shorts
and tank top combo, painted my Converse high-tops day-glow
green with yellow puff-paint squiggles, and sprayed my red
Mohawk with aerosol glitter, Brad created a full suit made
entirely from blonde thrift-store wigs that made him look
like the Cowardly Lion crossed with Cousin Itt from the
Addams Family, and Michael debuted his trademark Mad
Matron look by donning multiple clashing polyester frocks
and platform boots along with the short wigs and make-up
favored by sensible housewives in the early 1970s. Michael also
permanently changed his name to Diet (pronounced like the
thing you go on to lose weight), a combo of then-current
celebrities Princess Di and E.T., the extra-terrestrial.

The conventional wisdom of the day, endlessly trumpeted
by the media, had it that America was returning to "traditional values." Hippies, druggies, punks, gays, atheists,
feminists, and people with the bad taste not to be white and
affluent were served notice that the times they were a-changin'
. . . back to the sort of corny suburban conformity that only
ever really existed in TV sitcoms from the '50s. The apotheosis

of this counterrevolution was the presidency of cornball-in-chief Ronald Reagan, as a blandly amiable paterfamilias to preside over an un-ironically retro nation. New wave musicians reacted against this turn with an efflorescence of eccentricity: think Devo's flowerpot hats, Cyndi Lauper's deranged debutante look, David Byrne's really, really big suit, and all those New Romantics running around dressed like pirates, Zoot suiters, or *fin de siècle* dandies. The Popstitutes weren't trying to out-weird anyone, but these ambient cultural cues surely influenced our aesthetic.

Our first gig was for Brad's art opening at San Francisco's Southern Exposure Gallery. He'd filled the cavernous white-walled space with a two-story high wooden diorama of a homoerotic hell full of devilish nude men engaging in lewd acts while being engulfed by flames. What did he mean by this? No idea. The place lacked a stage or seating, so the three- or four-dozen people there just milled around waiting for us to perform. When we finally did, Diet grasped the mic and fixed the crowd with a gaze that instantly turned them into an audience. "Don Juaaaaan, I met him in Ringold Alleeeeey!"

Diet's voice was more theatrical than melodious, but his gestures, expressions, and intonations were those of a pro. I, on the other hand, immediately faced an appalling truth: something about the Popstitutes' sound deactivated my sense of rhythm. My vocals, button pushing, and dancing were all humiliatingly off-beat. I prayed my incompetence would go unnoticed in the cacophony but feared otherwise. The audience clapped noncommittally at the end of each song while staring at us with that bemused ennui typical of jaded urban sophisticates. Anticipating just this non-response, Diet had procured a few dozen overripe bananas for me to pass around at our finale. He invited the audience to hurl them at us (fruits for the fruits), subtly suggesting our terribleness was ironic. Afterward, Diet glowed with pleasure. "I think that went rather well!"

Our second show was serenading an acid orgy thrown by the Radical Faeries at a swank home in the Berkeley Hills. Our third was a guerilla gig at "Dorothy's House," a crumbling cement bunker out by a cruise-y gay nude beach. Both "audiences" were distracted from our performances by deeds of *l'amour*, but in between acts of depravity some guys would stop and watch us. Nobody tapped their toes, but they appeared to like us—nodding, smiling, and laughing when appropriate. True, the clapping at the end of songs was spotty and restrained, but to my ears it sounded sincere.

Even so, I didn't enjoy performing. I never mentioned this to Diet because I didn't want to rain on his parade. He very clearly *adored* performing. And what's more, his immersion in the creative process was making him nicer. Oh, he still went in for his "the trouble with you is . . ." character dissection rants, but with only half the venom. The band was already making the world a better place!

Chapter 14: Mike: 1987

THE MURKY BLUE INFINITUDE OF THE Pacific reminded me of death, so I turned and faced the beach, a sandy rock- and driftwood-strewn enclave ringed by hills covered in windswept pines and manzanitas. Perhaps a dozen guys were lying around in various states of undress, basking in some rare San Francisco sun. As I scanned the scene, a thoroughly naked boy sprawled on the sand a few yards away looked up, smiled coyly, and rose to his feet. He was slender, well proportioned, and wore his bleach-y blond hair down past his shoulders. This was wildly unfashion- able for gay guys, but judging from his serene poise, I guessed it signified confidence rather than cluelessness. The boy slipped on cutoff jeans and sneakers, cast a come hither look my way, and marched up a short hill into the scrubby wilderness. I followed him till we reached a small patch of level ground surrounded by bushes. He turned and faced me with smoldering brown eyes . . . cue train entering tunnel, champagne cork popping, fireworks, rocket lift-off, *et cetera*.

Afterward, we sat on a rock and talked. Mike was twenty-one, new to town from Seattle, and—as I'd surmised—the hair was on purpose. Mike was no cookie-cutter gayboy, but a devotee of Modern Primitivism, a post-punk trend incorporating body modification, kinky fetish-wear, edgy experimental literature, and screech-y industrial music. "At some point I might try to get a band together. Maybe start a club. You?"

I'd just graduated from U.C. Berkeley and gotten a busboy job at Café Flore, where I intended to work for a year before taking off to grad school . . . all of which sounded too boring to explain. "I'm in a band called the Popstitutes."

"Cool. We should hang out again sometime."

Not only did Mike and I "hang out" again, we began dating. By this I mean our lives devolved into a nonstop orgy of unnatural passion consummated mostly on the floor of the Tenderloin apartment where Mike was staying with friends. Since we were both looking for a place in the city, we decided to find one together. My brain suspected this was foolhardy as we'd only known each other three weeks, but that particular organ was not responsible for the decision. We quickly found a flat on Moss Street just off skid row with rooms so small they put me in mind of a dollhouse. We settled in along with Diet and some folks who don't enter into the story. Mike and I spent every night together and my fear of death by AIDS was buried under an avalanche of sexy delight.

Sexiness wasn't Mike's only appealing quality, though. He also possessed a *savoir vivre* I found infinitely alluring. Mike always knew about cool new bands the second they came out, introducing me to the enchanting sounds of Skinny Puppy, Laibach, and the Revolting Cocks, among others. He also took me to my first Vietnamese restaurant (still a rare thing in 1987), a place of such mouthwatering scrumptiousness I dream of it to this day. Best of all, Mike was both magnificently heedless and spontaneous. If he felt like doing something, he just *did* it.

By contrast, Diet and I never went to club or a protest, bought clothes, made friends, liked a band or a book, ate out, or did *anything* really without first deliberating to make sure we weren't being bourgeois, sentimental, conservative, superstitious, or any of the other things we were intent on not being. Having grown up Catholic, Diet was used to a slightly insane regimen of moral scrupulosity. In fact, he reveled in it. The possibility of falling into sin added drama to everyday life and gave him a chance to wield his keen intellect. I, on the other hand, found such scrupulosity exhausting, suffocating, and no fun. I deeply envied boys like Mike who swash-buckled their way through life, confident in their right to pursue happiness with nary a thought of how their actions resonated in some abstract pitched battle between good and evil.

And so, I fell wonderfully, madly, inescapably, and torrentially in love with Mike. Diet had always dismissed my conviction that romance was the key to happiness as so much balderdash, but Mike was proving him wrong. Not only was it sheer bliss to be with Mike, but the non-Mike-related aspects of my life became blissful too, so that my whole world sparkled with joy and possibility. Not only was love proving to be everything promised by the sappiest Girl Group songs from the 1960s, it was *better.*

Then one night, a couple of months after Mike and I had moved in together, Mike came home and composed his face into an approximation of regretful sadness. "Alvin . . . I, um, think we need to stop seeing so much of each other. You and I can still be friends, but you know . . ." He disappeared into his room while my heart shriveled into dust. How could I have thought a Love God like Mike could care for a schlump like me? I was a hideous, subhuman outcaste whom nobody would ever love *ever, ever, ever.* That night and every night thereafter I heard Mike and his new paramours through the paper-thin walls separating our rooms. This was not mere pedestrian grunting or moaning, mind you, but a full symphony of unrestrained passion.

"What do I do?" I asked Diet. "Without Mike, I'll die of miserableness."

Diet's eyebrows lifted sardonically. "You only want him because he's a guy's guy and you're a fey boy and you've swallowed the values of the patriarchy. It's the same tired story over and over: The idolized masculine rejects and is worshipped by the excluded feminine. Like in *Rocky Horror* with the femme-y Dr. Frank N. Furter running after the macho muscle monster or *Lost in Space* with queen-y old Dr. Smith chicken-hawking on wholesome young Will Robinson."

"Mike is pretty *boyish*," I concurred. "The other day we went to the park and it wasn't even all that hot out but he took his shirt off . . ."

"Typical exhibitionism for the narcissistic alpha-male," interjected Diet.

"Then he climbed a tree and swung on a low-hanging branch like a monkey. Then this big old shaggy dog ran up to us and he started *romping* with it."

"Romping?" Diet knit his brows in mock consternation. "The bitch must die."

"But I'm in love with him!"

Diet waved his hand dismissively. "It'll pass. You and Mike don't even have anything in common. Go find someone new and leave me be. I'm writing a new song."

I knew Diet actually liked Mike and was only dissing him for my sake, but he did have a point. Mike *was* magnificently male with an uncomplicated love of motorcycles, black leather, and tattoos. I, by contrast, liked bicycles, vintage blazers, and the caustic social satire of *Spy* magazine. We were horribly mismatched and my longing for him was a tired cliché. But that didn't make it stop. *Maybe,* I thought, *I'll butch up a little and see if that helps.* I splurged on a black leather motorcycle jacket and made an appointment at a nearby tattoo parlor.

Choosing an image to live with for the rest of my life, short though it might be, proved difficult. I wanted something purely decorative so that if my personality were to change, my tattoo wouldn't clash with the New Me. I'd seen enough responsible dads in YMCA locker rooms sporting bad-ass skull and crossbones to see the danger there. I also worried the meaning of my tattoo might change. The innocuous, if annoyingly saccharine, Smiley Face had recently been adopted by an immigrant-bashing, right wing political party in Sweden, no doubt forcing some poor Swede who'd gotten a Smiley Face tattoo during a fit of positive thinking into expensive and painful laser tattoo removal surgery. I needed a design both meaningless and certain to remain so. When I discovered the alchemical symbol for antimony (looks rather like a crossed trident), I decided it was a safe bet and immediately got it permanently affixed to my upper left arm.

When I showed my tattoo to Mike, he flashed me his recently perfected *sorry for breaking your heart* smile and pronounced it

"Rad." The way he used contemporary slang without irony or self-consciousness was *soooo* sexy! Then he went on, "Hey, didja hear? Boy Club is hiring go-go dancers. I'm starting next Wednesday. Pay's pretty good, too. Maybe you should apply. Gotta run, I have a date. See ya." *Argh!* Everyone I knew went to Boy Club at the I-Beam weekly so we could mush ourselves into the writhing human mass on the jam-packed dance floor while a few chosen go-go boys flaunted their shirtless bodies atop the speakers in demi-godly isolation. Mike working there absolutely confirmed that he existed on a higher plane than I.

And yet . . . I might not be conventionally handsome, but go-go dancing was *my* thing. Put on The Au Pairs, the Silicon Teens, or Our Daughter's Wedding and I became a tireless new wave dervish. The next day, clad in black boots and jeans, a sleeveless tee shirt, two studded-leather belts, two-dozen rubber bangle bracelets, and thin red suspenders, along with multiple necklaces, chains, and medallions à la Billy Idol, I presented myself to the man in charge of hiring at Boy Club. I'd expected to audition, but he took one look at my ensemble and said, "You'll do." A victory for maximalist accessorizing.

Now, I thought, *Mike will see I'm not to be tossed aside like a used condom!* Alas, he reacted to the news I'd be working alongside him with the same cheery indifference he'd shown my tattoo. "Great, we can share a taxi."

Go-go dancing proved every bit as fun as it looked in the movies. Staring across the dance floor crammed with vivacious youths painted pink and purple by flashing disco lights was fun to the point of sublime . . . *plus* I got free drinks. And the music was always perfecto, everything from mainstream groups like Erasure to unjustly obscure stuff like the Vicious Pink

Phenomena. When my first glorious night on the pedestal ended, I went backstage to change out of my sweat-drenched clothes and reemerged to see . . . Mike leaving with someone else.

That was it. I'd run out of ideas. Mike was *gone.* Over the next few months my heartbreak mutated into existential depression. Except for the four wondrous hours spent dancing at Boy Club each week, I hated my life. The world seemed dim, claustrophobic, and punishingly ugly, like the inside of a filthy, malodorous metal garbage can. My mind, formerly a carnival of mad fancies, became a morgue of discouraging apprehension. The immediate cause of my dejection was losing Mike, but The Plague wasn't helping. I kept seeing too-thin men with mauve lesions hobbling down the streets and my fears of an early demise returned with a vengeance. To keep my brain from thinking horrible thoughts I began guzzling booze and ingesting illicit narcotics with abandon.

Apparently, substance abuse is not an efficacious long-term strategy for grappling with life's difficulties (who knew?). Over the following six months my emotions yo-yoed between frosty white numbness and soul-crushing despair. I abandoned my plans for grad school (why bother when I and everyone I knew would be dying soon?), determining to live *in* and *for* The Moment. I succeeded, though unfortunately The Moment I was living *in* and *for* proved to be one of anguished torment. Then, a stroke of luck: my boss at the café fired me in the middle of a shift. Shocked and humiliated, I replaced narcotics with massive self-administered doses of Dead Can Dance, a hauntingly ethereal neo-medievalist Goth band whose music worked the occult miracle of transmogrifying my ugly agony into beautiful anguish. I pulled through.

In the meantime, Mike had risen like a star to become the It Boy of queer San Francisco. Now known as Michael Blue, he'd gotten a mohawk, started stripping at The Nob Hill Cinema, starred in a few porn films, and topped it all off by becoming a wildly popular DJ and club entrepreneur, first at Club Chaos, then Uranus. Flush with cash, he moved out of our flat and into a life that looked like one long tickertape parade in his honor. Mike's success made him more enviable, but—thanks to my lifelong habit of bitterly resenting winners—less lovable. What finally ended my obsession with Mike wasn't his social ascension, though, but an unconfirmed rumor.

Someone, I forget who, told me in strict confidence that Mike had slept with my idol, Marc Almond. As half of the synth-pop duo Soft Cell, and later a solo act, Almond's overwrought songs of anomie and heartbreak like "Tainted Love," "Waifs and Strays," and "Tears Run Rings" had provided the soundtrack for my life's romantic tragedies. The image of Marc with his sylphlike build, kinky fetish-wear, and gobbed-on eyeliner always lifted my spirits. He made me feel I wasn't some anonymous, anomalous loser, but one of the legion of Glamorously Doomed boys—the "gutter hearts"—for whom Marc sang his melancholy airs and ballads. I never bothered to find out if the rumor about Marc and Mike was true (I didn't really want to know), but the mental image of them together without *me* ignited a small explosion of indignation in my mind. How dare they! Envy might be one of the seven deadlies, but it did me a world of good, corroding love's sinister bonds and restoring my emotional equipoise.

Chapter 15: The Daily Bump 'n' Grind: 1987

NERVES AFLUTTER, I STOOD OUTSIDE THE Campus Theater looking up at the giant white, plastic marquee proclaiming LIVE NUDE BOYS! *Well,* I thought, *I'm a boy. I'm alive. And under my clothes I'm nude. I should qualify.* I pushed through the swinging doors into a small, dimly lit lobby. A hefty attendant in a white dress shirt sat in a ticket booth behind a Plexiglass window wearing a look of immeasurable boredom.

"Who do I see about working here?"

"I'm Stu," said the attendant. "You can talk to me."

"Well, first off . . . how much does it pay?"

"Thirty bucks a show, but you can double or triple that with tips."

"What about the hours?"

"Dancers perform one half-hour show a day."

"And what exactly would this show consist of?"

Stu looked me up and down appraisingly. "We've got one starting in a few minutes. Go on in and see if you think it's something you could do."

I pushed through another pair of swinging doors into the darkened movie theater. Scattered throughout the sea of plush red seats were a couple of dozen men transfixed by an enormous screen on which a comely lad was collecting for his paper route in rather unorthodox fashion. I took a seat in back and waited. Ten minutes later a red velvet curtain descended and Stu's voice crackled over the speaker system. "Gentlemen, it's time for our live show with Brandon! You're welcome to get intimate with the performer, but the city and county of San Francisco strictly forbids the touching genitals or buttocks. Tipping, however, is always greatly appreciated. And now, here's Brandon for your enjoyment."

Generic disco boomed, the curtain lifted, and a husky muscular fellow dressed in gym clothes bounded onto the stage with a bored look on his blunt, handsome face. He performed a few half-hearted hip swivels in time with the music then pulled off his all clothes, save for tennis shoes and socks, and proceeded to love himself up (if you catch my drift). Once Brandon was visibly in the mood for love (if you catch my drift), he hopped off the stage and moved through the audience, spending a minute or so hovering over each customer. The men would feel his legs or torso while hungrily staring at his privates and stuff tips into his socks. Once he'd finished working the audience, he returned to the stage and the show came to a climax (if you catch my drift). The audience clapped and the curtain fell. The whole thing lasted perhaps twenty minutes.

I returned to the front and told Stu I possessed the required job skills.

"You want to audition?"

Unlike prostitution or promiscuity, stripping was entirely public. One foot on that stage would forever mark me as a disreputable character, the sort respectable people called a *sleaze*. On the other hand . . . I didn't know any respectable people and my workday would be a mere thirty minutes long. And, I had to face it, some quirk of my psychic constitution rendered the strictures of ordinary jobs insufferable to me. Restaurant work felt like a cross between the treadmill at the gym and one of those Japanese game shows on which contestants are abused and humiliated in front of a sadistic audience. Office work was even worse, calling to mind those B movies in which some poor soul—bound and gagged, but eyes wide with terror—is slowly walled up brick-by-brick in the dungeon of some damp, rat-infested Transylvanian castle.

"Sure, I'll audition."

"Follow me," said Stu. He led me to grim little room with a mirror and saggy couch. "I'll put you right on. Try and have fun with it, and be sure to wipe up the stage after your show. Good luck!"

Before I had time for second thoughts the movie stopped, the curtain fell, and Stu introduced me as a special guest performer. I ran onto the stage, the music began, and the curtain lifted. Showtime! I busted out a few dance moves while surveying the audience. Dark though it was, I could just make out the faces of the men staring up at me—a bunch of Regular Joes ranging in age from late twenties to late sixties, most wearing business suits, a few with their business out (if you catch my drift). In most social situations I was painfully shy. It took me thirty minutes and three drinks just to work up enough nerve to say hi to cute boys in bars. Thankfully, though, my brain did not process this as a social situation. It just said, *The heck with this!* and shut off. I danced around and took off my shirt, danced around and removed my belt, danced around and shimmied out of my jeans, danced around and—moment of truth—shimmied out of my underwear. *Ta-da!* Live Nude Boy!

Truthfully, I half expected the audience to stalk out en masse, or at least wander off. I wasn't especially young or buffed and from certain angles my prominent nose and weak chin made me look like a fish. But, to my infinite relief, the men remained in their seats ogling lustfully. I quickly apprehended (on a fuzzy, sub-verbal level) that sexiness was less a matter of physical beauty than a performance—something done with hips and eyes, and something I could do every bit as well as the next strumpet. As my initial anxiety subsided I found being the center of attention titillating. Suddenly I was *in the mood* (if you catch my drift). The men responded to this with a perceptible increase in excitement. I gleefully hopped off the stage to work them for tips. Getting pawed and petted didn't bother me a whit, and I quite liked the way my socks filled with bills as I made my way down the aisles—a process that reminded me of bees gathering pollen. After twenty minutes I returned to the stage for my finale and finished up to respectable applause.

"You're hired!" said Stu.

Tradition decreed that strippers get a gimmick, and mine was actually dancing. The customers might be happy to settle for ostentatious onanism, but I whirled around the stage like a coked-up backup dancer on an MTV video. When disrobing, I didn't just *remove* my clothes but *flung* them off with wild abandon, all except for my undies, which I swung around over my head in time with my theme song, "You Spin Me Round (Like a Record)" by Dead or Alive.

In old movies featuring showgirls, there's always a great scene in the dressing room where the girls sit in front of mirrored vanities and trade catty comments while powdering their faces and lacing their bustiers.

"Lend me your eye shadow, will ya honey?"

"Aw, buy your own!"

"Miss Snootypuss thinks now she's got herself a big butter 'n' egg man she's somethin' special."

"Way your fella was lookin' at me earlier you might wanna tighten your leash, girl."

"You tarts just keep your mitts offa him, hear me?"

At The Campus we generally used the dressing room one at a time, but even during the weekly group shows (five dancers at once) I never witnessed any such drama. Everyone just talked about clubs, TV shows, new potato chip flavors . . . boring stuff. True, a few boys went in for competitive braggadocio, regaling us with tales of their lovers' largesse or how much they bench-pressed at the gym, but we never fought over men or hurled hairbrushes at one another.

I enjoyed group shows because I got to make out with the other dancers, most of whom I found flesh-quiveringly sexy. We'd start out frozen into an erotic *tableau vivant* before coming to life for a mock orgy. After a couple of minutes, we'd all pour off stage to work the audience at once. Speaking of the other dancers, people often think of strippers as being prostitutes, psychologically unbalanced, uneducated, druggy, and pathologically promiscuous, but I can happily report that few of us were ever more than one of these things at a time. Weirdly, a few of the guys were totally straight and had to spread girlie magazines around on the stage while they danced to arouse themselves. I could never understand how they stood being pawed by men. On those rare occasions a woman came to the theater (usually dragged there by a pervy husband) I found it difficult to stay focused on the task at hand (if you catch my drift) while she fondled me. Once, when a busload of giggling female Japanese tourists swarmed into the theater, I actually turned and fled the stage.

We "dancers" measured our marketability and, I fear, our self-worth, with tips. Most men put bills in our socks in such a way that we couldn't see the denomination, and most such mystery bills bore the face of George Washington. If a customer was handing out fives, tens, or twenties he usually made sure you saw so you'd give him more pawing time. The highly sexy got lots of big bills; the less sexy, fewer. It's actually a bit of a mystery how many guys were in the former category as dancers were notorious braggarts and liars. And yet, after group shows when we were all in the dressing room together, certain guys always removed a lot of big bills from their socks, so we all had a pretty good grasp of our relative market value. Me—I was low to middling.

The biggest drawback to The Campus was that dancers were required to do one show every day for six weeks followed by one week off. This left me feeling positively *married* to the place. Wanting to keep some sexual energy for myself, I switched to The Nob Hill Cinema, where dancers only did four shows a week, and where Mike still worked. It meant finding a second part-time job, but that felt like something I could face. What I wasn't sure of was if I could face Mike. Passing him in the lobby would be OK, but The Nob Hill also put on group shows. How would it feel to be thrust into XXX action with The Man That Got Away?

Soon enough I found out. We started the show on opposite ends of the stage, but during the course of our theatrical groping and grinding I accidentally-on-purpose wound up next to him. Mike could've ignored me, but instead he threw his arm around my shoulder, comradely as you please, and pulled me in for a long sensuous kiss. A jolt of sexual energy charged through my body leaving me with a hot, empty, lighter-than-air feeling. I half expected to float away like a balloon. Then he turned his affections to another dancer and I felt . . . OK. Well, jealous and melancholy, sure . . . but there was no operatic heartbreak. What a relief!

I never told my family about stripping, but I never hid it from anyone else. A lot of gay men, my pals more than most, were wholly uninfected by middle-class morality; they regarded strippers and hustlers not as sad, marginalized victims, but adorably self-reliant little scamps. Stripping probably *added* to my allure. And it didn't hurt that sex work and porn were just then becoming chic, if not *de rigueur*, amongst queer-theory reading activists and academics. Attend a smart-set party and at some point you'd hear a symphony of beepers going off, summoning all the rent boys to their assignations.

As for the sex workers' rights movement, I had mixed feelings. Sure, the stigma around selling sex was antiquated and irrational, but I suspected that if sex work were to become respectable it wouldn't pay nearly as well.

I did have a cause, though: I wanted to eroticize counterculture dissidence. I'd just seen an amazing drag version of Genet's *The Balcony* and was exploring all sorts of theories about the psycho-sexual underpinnings of political authority. So, although the management suggested I choose a look from their tired roster of cash-clinching clichés—jock, sailor, college boy, construction worker—I insisted on stripping from the same new wave outfits I wore to Boy Club. I got away with this because the customers barely noticed anyone's clothes. Their sexual triggers were fleshly, not semiotic, with a strong focus on just what you'd expect.

Most patrons dutifully obeyed the injunction against touching my nether regions and for the few desperadoes who didn't, a light slap on the hand was enough to discourage further transgressions. I did not, at the time, realize this gentlemanly reserve was a temporary anomaly caused by the AIDS terror. I'd only been at the Nob Hill a little while before that terror manifested itself in a new and peculiar way when Mr. Prescott, the florid-faced, silver-haired owner/manager, convened the employees for an important announcement. In his nasal-y carnival-barker's voice he informed us he'd conferred with his lawyers and discovered that, "The way the law is written, it's perfectly legal for the patrons to touch you boys *anywhere*, provided they wear rubber gloves so there's no flesh-on-flesh contact." To facilitate this, he was instituting a new feature called "Boy in A Box."

The set-up involved two adjacent boxes, each the size of a telephone booth (for younger readers, that's about 2-½ feet deep, 2-½ feet wide) with a glass partition between them. Each side had a phone so the customer could call the dancer and issue requests: show me your whatever. And, embedded in the middle of the glass, there'd be a pair of gloves. Men could stick their hands into them and feel the "Boy in A Box" much the way lab workers handle radioactive isotopes. I and the other dancers protested that we had *zero* interest in this, but Mr. Prescott decreed we spend at least half an hour in The Box after each show, like it or lump it. "Besides," he added, "they'll be paying for this by the minute and half the money's yours."

I approached my first foray into the box with great trepidation, but was still unprepared for the reality. I am not an especially kinky person, let alone a rubber fetishist, but had the rubber gloves been black, I might have been able to convince myself they were sexy. People encased in black rubber look mean, invulnerable, and sadistic—it's a sexual archetype. Not my thing, but I understand it. The gloves in the booth, however, were not black but the thin yellow type commonly sold at supermarkets. They brought to mind not some S&M Rubber Master lording over his dungeon, but Mom in the kitchen washing up after dinner. I'd never found being sexually objectified degrading or unpleasant. Rather, I find NOT being sexually objectified degrading and unpleasant. But being boxed, however, felt dehumanizing in a way the upstairs shows never had. Upstairs I felt like an exotic dancer. Downstairs, I felt like a dirty dish.

Fortunately, the customers didn't much care for the whole Boy in A Box deal either. Why would they when, for the same money they could pick up hustler on Polk Street and skip the dishwashing gloves? After a couple of irritating months, the program was discontinued. I then settled happily into my new career, delighted that the short hours allowed me so much time for club-hopping, the Popstitutes, and my favorite sports activity, reading in bed.

Chapter 16: Ring, Ring!

THOUGH I EARNED ENOUGH AT THE Nob Hill for essentials like hair dye, cocktails, and taxicabs, I still needed cash for luxuries like food and rent. Hoping it wouldn't utterly deplete me of *joie de vivre*, I took a job with Diet at a phone room selling tickets for a wildly uneven theater company. I know, *I know*. You *hate* telemarketers. They call in the middle of dinner or your favorite television show. They're pushy and deceitful and thoroughly irritating. I felt the same way and was thoroughly ashamed of myself. Working only four hours a night Sundays through Thursdays, however, was such a perfect fit with my pathologically indolent lifestyle that I couldn't refuse.

Located next door to a Japanese import-export company with a doorway flanked on either side by murals of Santa Claus and Godzilla, the telemarketing office consisted of gray cubicles set in a musty, airless room with a moldy rug and glaring fluorescent lights. The pay was lousy and the benefits nonexistent, but I didn't care. Working alongside Diet made the breaks almost as fun as hanging out at a really boring nightclub, plus nobody cared if I came to work with purple hair. Throw in free coffee and Lipton's Instant Soup Mix at the snack station and you can see why someone with no ambition and a tenuous grasp on reality might find the job acceptable.

The big drawback was that I had to beg, pester, cajole, and wheedle total strangers, suburban matrons mostly, into seeing plays I myself would have paid not to see. We telemarketers often joked about just how bad the shows could be. For every hit there were two stinkers that had patrons running for the exits. The ticketholders always came back, though, because we obsequious, oleaginous, unctuous telemarketers would phone up and remind them how very important theater was to *Culture*. We played to their snobbery, telling them how superior they were to their neighbors, slack-jawed watchers of television and philistine moviegoers. They fell for it again and again. This season's shows would be better. This year the life-changing potential of *Drama* would be fully realized, and Western Civilization would remain safe from the depredations of mass media vulgarity. We'd hang up the receiver after each successful hoodwinking and laugh, "I got a sale!"

Most of my co-workers were office-hacks trying to pay off credit card debts with temporary second jobs. They dressed neatly and kept up a joke-y workplace patter like secondary characters on a TV sit-com. And yet, under close observation I detected quiet desperation lurking beneath their cheery exteriors. It manifested with inappropriately bitter little comments about video store late fees and a certain glassy-eyed look that said, "My life is an exhausting repetition of tedious chores, alienated labor, and empty entertainments." I couldn't pity them though, because they lacked the humility to admit they were miserable. The professional telemarketers, on the other hand, were adorably kvetch-y and eccentric: cynical British expats, psychedelic slackers, autodidactic intellectuals, and devotees of hopelessly geeky pass-times like the Renaissance Pleasure Faire or Cigar Box Guitars. Among my favorites were Miriam and Alain.

Miriam was an octogenarian Jewish radical with a penchant for jarringly girlish pink polyester pants suits. She wanted to form a union, but never got anywhere because we were all magnificently expendable. She'd interrupt our manager's annoyingly positive weekly pep-talks to ask, in her gravelly New York accent, "Now, why is it exactly workers are paid by the sale in this operation? If what we do is valuable, shouldn't we be paid twenty-five dollars an hour?" The economics of this were absurd, but she'd go on and on until the manager grew frustrated and sent us back to work. If she hadn't been the top-seller in the room I'm sure they'd have fired her. Despite the fierce rhetoric, Miriam exuded a motherly quality, always noticing if someone looked thin or wasn't dressed warmly enough. I suspect her communistic vision grew less out of a rage against social injustice than a frustrated desire to force-feed chicken soup to everyone in the world. In a culture where most people mellow with age, I looked up to her as a shining example of recalcitrant feistiness.

Alain (probably an "Allen" who'd changed his name back when it was fashionable for gay men to put on airs), was an elderly, old-school queen who'd frittered away a small fortune on boys and booze on "the continent" and was living in "reduced circumstances." He'd show up at work dressed for an *al fresco* dinner party on the Amalfi coast circa 1962 in pedal pushers, sandals, and blousy white shirts unbuttoned halfway to the navel. "I find clothes so terribly *confiiining*!" he'd say in his affected, upper crust drawl. He loved to reminisce and called young boys "*dollyvoos*," which just floored me. Alain couldn't make a sale to save his life and some conjectured the management kept him around for comic relief. Despite his ridiculousness, the fact Alain had made it into his sixties without surrendering, or even toning down, his fabulous pretensions cheered me to no end.

All sales jobs are tough, but phone sales are the worst. You repeat the same pitch fifty or a hundred times a night, night after night, until your brain feels ready to explode. People slam the phone down on you or chew you out for interrupting "family time" or call you vile names, but being rude back is grounds for dismissal. Equally annoying are patrons who act like your best friend. They'll drone on about how they can't spare a few hundred dollars for the holiday fund to bring orphans to see *A Christmas Carol* because they just went over-budget on their Brazilian vacation or spent a hundred thousand dollars remodeling their kitchen. The burnout factor hit me about two weeks into the job. I wanted to quit, but instead just grit my teeth and fantasized about hunting down the more disagreeable patrons with a bazooka.

According to the esteemed gurus of self-help and inspiration, one ought never indulge in regret because everything is a learning experience and an opportunity for personal growth. Be that as it may, I regret every second I spent at that soul-sucking drudgery. Even while working there I knew it was a mistake I'd rue for the rest of my days.

Chapter 17: Four Blonds 1984–1986

ROBERT WAS ALWAYS THE FIRST PERSON at a party to start dancing on the furniture. Put on "Freethinker" by Voice Farm and—*boom!*—he'd be up on the kitchen table doing the Watusi. Robert was always ready for the next joke, the next game, the next nightclub. Like some madcap heiress from an old movie, he made inexhaustible exuberance seem not just fun, but terribly smart and classy. Though he didn't do drag, I always picture him in my mind's eye wearing a Holly Golightly-style black cocktail dress toasting the moon with a glass of pink champagne. His being the fifteen-zillionth gayboy to adopt flamboyantly camp mannerisms could have been tiresome, but wasn't. Robert's large, slightly bulgy brown eyes acted as counter-ballast to his frivolousness, staring out at the world with sincere good will, curiosity, and a faint suggestion of nameless dread. I liked Robert.

Once, I asked him out on a date. My brilliant idea of a romantic time was attending a speech by vice presidential candidate, Geraldine Ferraro. Afterward, he agreed with all my theories about female supremacy, but somehow failed to melt into my arms. We stayed friends, though, and over the next few years I was forever running into him out on the town, kicking up his heels at discos, adding his nasal cackle to the roar of clubs, and glamorizing the streets with his chic little outfits. (Even in the New Romantic era he was one of very few boys who could successfully work a bolero jacket.) After a couple of years, though, I started to see him around less often, then less often than that, and then finally, he seemed to have vanished.

I soon recieved confirmation of Robert's untimely demise.

Shortly after, I went on a date with Dave. Unlike most boys I knew, Dave didn't have a big personality so I don't remember much about him other than that his whole body, normally a milky white, turned bright scarlet in the throes of passion. A few days after our date, I ran into him on the street wearing only a pair of tiny shorts and a healthy glow. He told me he'd just jogged a full hour and felt gloriously invigorated. Only days later I heard the flabbergasting news he'd passed away.

When I woke up with red spots all over my arms, I immediately thought: Karposi's sarcoma. I'd been expecting it, but even so the shock gave me vertigo. I felt terrified, but also weirdly calm. My wait was over. The end had come. Riding the bus to the doctor's office, the perpetual chatter that usually clogs my brain shut off and everything seemed more vividly *there* than it ever had before. Objects were more solid, the sun sunnier, the air airier. My doctor quickly determined the red spots were only chicken pox. This wasn't a permanent reprieve; there was no test for AIDS and I might still get *sick* at any moment. All the same I was overcome with rapturous relief, as if I'd been handed a second life.

I squealed with delight when an acquaintance told me I had a secret admirer: Little Benji, a rosy-cheeked munchkin who'd recently resigned his position as the trophy boyfriend of a minor local rock star. I asked Benji out and we went to a Singaporean restaurant, then a movie, then my place. He spent every second complaining about his ex but I didn't care because Benji was the cutest thing this side of the plush toy department at FAO Schwarz. I didn't know whether to take him to bed or serve him pretend tea with some dollies and teddy bears. I called up for a second date but kept getting his answering machine. I wasn't even surprised when our mutual acquaintance told me he was at SF General, dying.

When I'd first moved to town at seventeen, I'd thought of San Francisco as a huge playground. Mystery lurked around every corner and the city twinkled with enchantment. Walking along hilly streets, I'd gazed up at the drawn curtains of apartment blocks to imagine vivid tableaus of glamour and excitement inside—soignée cocktail parties, beautiful people involved in torrid love affairs, *avant gardists* founding new schools of art. Gradually, the ever-increasing pall of death replaced these fantasies with visions of bedridden young men whose eyes stared into the next world.

Then I hooked up with a lad named Muffin. Within moments of our first meeting, we ran off to a no-tell motel, stopping only for a pint of whiskey. Without planning, we'd run into each a couple times a year and instantly slip away together. Our encounters were so random and intermittent I didn't really notice when he stopped turning up, but a few years after he'd gone missing I caught sight of him walking across the street. At first I didn't recognize him as his face was half-purpled and he was using a cane. I considered running over to say, "Hi, remember me?" but didn't because what would I say next? "Nice sodomizing you, sorry you're dying." I took the easy way out and fled, silently promising to forever after think of myself as a terrible person.

My friends were a restless lot, always moving. In 1980 when someone disappeared I assumed he'd transplanted to New York, gone off to college, or, at worst, relocated to the suburbs to lead a life of dull mediocrity. A few years later my default assumption was that the missing person had died. There used to be a joke: What are the three fastest means of communication? Telephone, television, and tell a queen. Despite knowing my fair share of queens, I'm not sure I was notified about every death. I heard about Jim, who'd been into video back when that word sounded so modern and thrilling, and Terry, the gentlemanly pornographer, but what of the others? How many people who'd faded out of my life had faded out of life itself? And if *everyone else* was dying, why was *I* starting to feel like a ghost?

I dreaded reading the obituaries in the *B.A.R.*, the local, free, gay paper. First, I flipped through the personal ads in back to see which of my friends were turning tricks. Then I'd skim the news, always the exact same few stories: someone discriminated against a gay, someone said gays were OK, an election was good for gays, an election was bad for gays, someone held a charity auction for something gay, some gay guy had been named Mr. Gay Something-or-other in a gay charity pageant. After that I perused the columns, reviews, letters to the editor, and events calendar. Only with every possible diversion exhausted would I turn to the obits. I never learned of a friend's death there, but I often recognized faces from around town and once saw someone I'd kissed a week before at a Christmas party.

How depressing that San Francisco, the only place in America routinely compared to Paris and The Emerald City, was now a somber and subdued zone of half-empty nightclubs and bars. How tiresome that one could now only have sex through rubber and plastic. How gruesome that straight America now found us homos pitiable or disgusting rather than charming or funny. And how unfair that so many people who'd played supporting roles in the unfolding drama of my life were getting dragged off stage in mid performance. If all my friends died, who would be around to help me recall the glorious exploits of my youth when I reached old age?

Except (*oh, right!*) I probably wouldn't reach old age—I'd be dying soon myself. The reasoning part of my brain *knew* this, but avoided thinking about it with ironclad discipline. I never once envisioned what I'd look like writhing with pain on a hospital gurney, imagined a tearful last farewell with my mom, or wondered what they'd say about me at my funeral. Epic though it was, my denial did not set my mind at ease. A barely submerged terror of death fouled my moods and troubled my sleep, leaving me enervated and angst-ridden.

In those days there was an oft-repeated film quote, "Live fast, die young, and leave a good-looking corpse!" When put on refrigerator magnets or novelty postcards it was meant to be funny, a quintessential example of overwrought B-movie dialogue. My friends and I giggled at the melodramatic phrasing, but we truly identified with the devil-may-care sentiment. We were youngsters and contemptuous not only of aging, but of the aged. When older gay guys dared show their saggy baggy faces at our revels, we looked right through them. Why not check out altogether before joining that sad fraternity of wrinkled wraiths haunting the scenes of their former glory? And yet . . . as more and more of my social set succumbed to The Plague (leaving corpses more ravaged than beautiful), I found the idea of living to a ripe old age ever more appealing. So what if my corpse had wrinkles? There's no law saying one *must* have an open-casket funeral. True, if I went on living, I'd eventually be forced to give up nightlife and do without the tender affections of beautiful young men, but I could always get a cat.

If a world without *me* was too terrible to imagine, I did occasionally contemplate a world without people *like* me. It seemed like kooky queens were dying faster than anyone else and that the art of maintaining a Deliciously Madcap Sensibility might soon be lost. (A strong visual memory here of gigantic Michael Benbrook bursting into The Stud dressed in a glitzy blue sequined socialite gown and a floor-length coat composed of sewn-together teddy bears.) Even when months went by in which nobody I knew died, some queer celebrity was sure to pass away: Klaus Nomi, Keith Haring, Liberace. It became all too easy to envision a future in which gay men were virtually extinct, reduced to the quasi-mythical status of druids or surrealists. My friends and I were still in our twenties when we started greeting each other after prolonged absences with a surprised, "Wow, *you're still alive!*"

Chapter 18: Antinomy

WHENEVER ANYONE ASKED WHAT MY TATTOO meant, I'd say, "It's the symbol for antimony, a metal used by medieval alchemists." Then, seeing the perplexity on my questioner's face, I'd add, "Alchemy was the science of turning lead into gold, only it didn't work." In this way the tattoo I'd hoped to be meaningless accidentally became a symbol of human futility. This didn't actually bother me as that fit rather well with my affectation of world-weary cynicism.

Then, one day while walking down Market Street, I ran into Spencer, my old non-Sugar Daddy from New York. He looked the same, but told me he'd been stricken with the plague, given up lawyering, and was visiting San Francisco as part of his new project: placing art in AIDS hospices. After chatting a bit, he asked about my tattoo. I tried to tell him it was a symbol for antimony but, inadvertently and without noticing, interposed the n and m so that I actually said antinomy, a different word altogether.

"I've heard of that!" said Spencer. "It's a moral paradox involving innately incompatible values. Freedom and equality, spontaneity and efficiency, justice and mercy . . . they're all good, but increase one and you diminish the other."

I tried to process this. "So not only is humanity doomed to fall short of its ideals, even our ideals are doomed to fall short of our ideals?"

Spencer nodded. "More or less."

"But surely one can find a happy balance," I countered.

Spencer wheezed a little, like someone with bad lungs. "But everyone weights these values differently so nobody's happy balance is the same. Every personal or social advance from one perspective can be a setback from a different but equally valid point of view."

"But," I objected, "every change either adds or subtracts from the sum total of human happiness."

Spencer shook his head. "But happiness is just one value and it can conflict with others. I mean, would a society where everyone was happy but produced *no* art be better than a society where everyone was miserable but produced beautiful art? There's no right answer."

I swallowed hard, fully grokking the horror. "Then there can never be a Utopia."

"Not one that everyone agrees is Utopian, no," said Spencer. "Nice tattoo, though."

We parted with vague promises to do lunch and I was left to contemplate the fact that I now *hated* my tattoo. That one can't turn lead into gold had never bothered me, but that one can't take the lead of humanity and create a golden millennium did. Despite my veneer of cynicism, I was actually a good 20th century liberal. I believed humanity was on a long, slow march toward the best of all possible worlds.

The evidence for this was spotty, but I'd watched so many old movies I couldn't conceive of a story not turning out well in the final reel. My imagination was thoroughly stunted, though I'd like to think in a nice way—like a bonsai tree. How, then, was I to reconcile my newfound intellectual pessimism with my emotional faith in happy Hollywood endings? The answer was obvious: I would not think of humanity as hopeless, but—like me—Glamorously Doomed. In an act of existential jiu-jitsu, humanity could find fun in its futile search for an unattainable utopia.

Some time later, while browsing the dictionary, I discovered my mistake in confusing antimony with antinomy. My tattoo was not a symbol for antinomy, the philosophical term Spencer referred to, but antimony, which really is just a metal of absolutely no use in turning lead into gold. My tattoo was meaningless after all. A Happy Ending, for me and my tattoo anyway. Spencer, on the other hand, died of AIDS.

Jennifer Blowdryer *Photo © Annie Sprinkle*

Diet Popstitute as Fashion Victim.
Left: *Photo © Gwyn Waters.*
Above: *Photo © Archives of Alvin Orloff*

Below: Mike Blue
Photo © Lewis Walden

Above: Alvin Orloff
Photo © Gwyn Waters

Alvin Orloff on the set of an
XXX film, May 19, 1990
Photo © Daniel Nicoletta

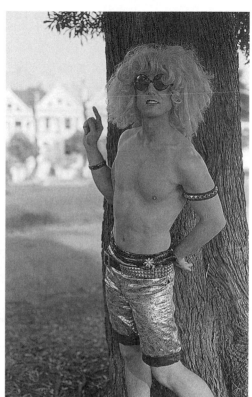

More Popstitutes.
Photos © Gwyn Waters

Club Chaos and Klubstitute "Heels on Wheels" (aka "The Homocore Float")
contingent in the SFLGBT Pride Parade, June 25, 1989. *Photo © Daniel Nicoletta*

The Wedding of Dina Fruitfly Popstitute to Zeon Popstitute Klubstitute
at the Crystal Pistol bar on Valencia, January 2, 1990. From left:
Danielle Willis, Bad Popstitute, Veronica Klaus, Stephen Maxxxine,
Zeon Popstitute, Phillip R. Ford, Dina (Fruitfly) Popstitute, Diet Popstitute,
Alvin Orloff, Tony Vaguely. *Photo © Daniel Nicoletta*

Jerome Caja on a cross. *Photo © Lewis Walden*

Justin Vivian Bond
Photo © Kip Duff

Mike Blue and Lewis
Photo © Lewis Walden

Stephen Maxxxine
Photo © Lewis Walden

The cast of *Vegas in Space*
Photo © Robin Clark

Phillip R.Ford
Photo © Rico Schwartzberg

Clockwise from top:
Leigh Crow (Elvisherselvis) and
Justin Vivian Bond wedding at
Klubstitute, Nov. 23, 1991;
Scorchy (aka Keith Klippensteen)
at Klubstitute, Nov. 23, 1991;
Bambi Lake, on the set of
Marc Huestis and Lawrence Helman's
documentary film "Sex Is",
March 9, 1991.
Photos © Daniel Nicoletta

Elvis Herselvis with Johnny Kat;
Klubsitute performers The Pleshettes, from
left: Tony Vaguely, Deena Davenport, Elvis
Herselvis, aka Leigh Crow, and Zeon
Photos © Kip Duff

Klubstitute regulars, clockwise from top: Deena Davenport *(Photo © Alvin Orloff)*; Brigit Brat, aka God's Girlfriend *(Photo © Kip Duff)*; Tyler Ingolia with Jerome Caja; Tina Gerhardt and Tyler Ingolia *(Photos © Tyler Ingolia)*

Clockwise from top:
Klubstitute regulars Tony Vaguely,
Diet Popstitute, and Alvin Orloff
(Photo © Daniel Nicoletta);
Tony Vaguely as Carrie
(Photo © Marc Geller);
Diet and Zeon
(Photo by Gwyn Waters);
Tony telling fortunes
(Photo by Gwyn Waters)

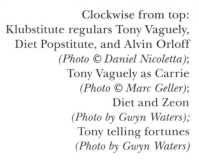

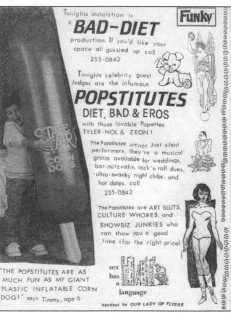

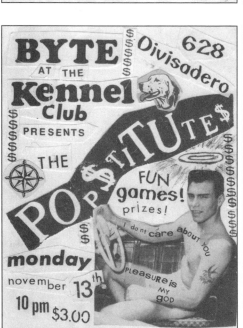

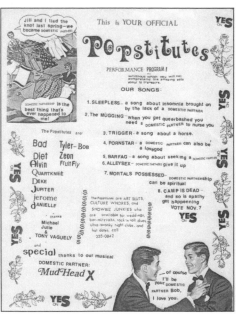

Popstitute flyers.
All flyers © Archives of Alvin Orloff

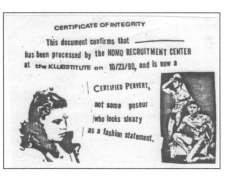

CERTIFICATE OF INTEGRITY

This document confirms that _____
has been processed by the HOMO RECRUITMENT CENTER
at the KLUBSTITUTE on 10/23/90, and is now a

CERTIFIED PERVERT,
not some poseur
who looks sleazy
as a fashion statement.

KLUBSTITUTE

Queer Niteclub and Cabaret with M.C. Diet Popstitute

NOW TUESDAYS AT THE STUD, PRESENTS

Birdie's Beatnik Bongo Night

With your Host-Chick
Birdie!

D.J.s Drew
Macaroni and Cheese
&
Alvin A Go Go
$3 Cheap!

TUESDAY, MARCH 8TH
THE STUD - 9TH & HARRISON

KLUBSTITUTE TUESDAY september 4
842 VALENCIA / between 19 & 20th
AT THE CRYSTAL PISTOL only 98 cents

D.J. Don BAIRD

Blowdryer & set

PERFORMANCE and
A BON VOYAGE PARTY
for the talented but lazy tearful
Jennifer Blowdryer

KATHLEEN
WOOD
AUTHOR OF
THE TENDERLOIN
ROSE

fortunetelling
by
Tony Vaguely

TUESDAY
JULY 24

New Performance By MICHAEL RICHARD

Bewitching Siren OMEWENNE

"Straight" From Telegraph Ave.—
BONK

Post-Musical D.J. AL-X

Instrumental Recital By ERIC BEGKVIST And
FRED LONBERG-HOLM

KLUBSTITUTE
Kwefent of Art & Discipline
842 VALENCIA / between 19 & 20th
AT THE CRYSTAL PISTOL only 98 CENTS

QUESTIONS? BOOKSTORE? CALL 550-2338
ALL - 7-VENUE

HALLOWEEN
AT KLUBSTITUTE

KLUBSTITUTE
Kwefent of Art & Discipline
THE CRYSTAL PISTOL
842 Valencia @ 20th
3 ULTRA-HOT BANDS

plus
D.O.J.
Remix
&
von Popstitute

Jack Acid
THE A.V.
MYTchell
BroThers
and
Special
Forces

TUESDAY
AUGUST 7

98 ¢

TUES.
MAY
15 9th

KEITH KNIGHT

KLUBSTITUTE
THE CRYSTAL PISTOL   842 Valencia @ 20th

JOIN the
Wed. Dec 4
HOLLYWOODLAWN
SQUARES

HOLLY WOODLAWN
Trash Star Enthroned and in the Flesh!!!
Klubstitute
175 Valencia @ Hara New World   Show 10:00 PM—Sharp!

★ KLUBSTITUTE
every tuesday
at The Crystal Pistol 842 Valencia

INTERESTING ART

STRANGE PERFORMANCES

A new and fascinating spectacle every week

QUEER ACTIVITIES

Funky

UNUSUAL MUSIC & VIDEO

The last Tuesday of every month is OUT OF ORDER for poetry and spoken word.
won't make you drowsy.

THIS TUESDAY
AUGUST 9TH 6-9 PM
GALA ART OPENING & ARTIST RECEPTION
"THE PHOENIX RISING FROM THE ASHES"
MISS KITTY LITTER-GREEN

EICHELBERGER'S
RESTAURANT / CABARET / BAR
2742 17TH ST.
@ FLORIDA ST., S.F., CA.
NO COVER   EICHELBERGER'S 863-4177
PLEASE NOTE CHANGE OF DATE

KLUBSTITUTE
THE CRYSTAL PISTOL
842 Valencia @ 20th

TUESDAY
AUGUST 21

98 ¢

JOSHUA'S WYMYNHOOD—A FEMME PEICE
featuring a bevy of beauties in an
outdoor dance performance

SENSITIVITY
A NEW VIDEO
BY SHAWN

sincere, real, and beautiful
music night with dj Remix

hot towel boy
Matthew JAMES

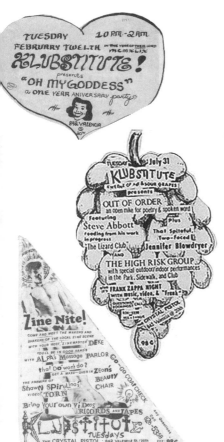

Klubstitute Flyers. *All flyers © Archives of Alvin Orloff*

Diet Popstitute,
Castro Street Fair, Oct. 1, 1989
Photo © Daniel Nicoletta

Tribute to Diet Popstitute Poster
(© Archives of Alvin Orloff)

Chapter 19: Porn Moguls

EXOTIC DANCERS ARE FREQUENTLY RECRUITED TO star in dirty movies and I was no exception. Legendary gay porn pioneer Toby Ross offered to fly me down to the San "Pornando" Valley to film *Tough Guys Do Dance*. (The title was a take off on literary bad-boy Norman Mailer's universally reviled film, *Tough Guys Don't Dance*.) I jumped at the chance since it paid nearly two weeks' salary for a single day's work. I didn't have to worry about safety as the gay porn world had firmly embraced condoms, it being universally assumed that any gayboy slutty enough to do porn was surely HIV positive. Toby paired me with a cartoonishly handsome guy (cleft chin, cheekbones, abs . . . the whole shebang) whose *nom de smut* was Lon Flexxx. *Ooh la la!*

Lon played a tipsy bon vivant wearing a tuxedo who, for reasons I forget, wanders into an apartment where I'm sleeping naked on a bed. Transfixed by my he-manliness, he falls to his knees and . . . well, use your imagination. I wake in the middle of this sexiness and I—offended that my hetero status has been compromised by a nocturnal blowjob—growl, "I've killed for less!" Not having seen the film, I was shocked to read in *The B.A.R.* review that my voice had been dubbed over by someone who sounded like George Peppard (you know, the guy who starred opposite Audrey Hepburn in *Breakfast at Tiffany's*). I was also slightly miffed that they referred to me as "scary Caligula look-alike Alvin Eros" though they sort of made up for it by also calling me a highlight.

After the shoot, Lon suggested that if I wanted more film work I ought to hook up with his agent. A few months later on an L.A. vacation, I called and got myself invited to the agent's house, a pleasant cottage nestled on a leafy side street of some Hollywood hill. Mr. Agent answered the door in white tennis shorts and a white polo shirt. His broad smile revealed frighteningly enormous white teeth and his head sported a stiff helmet of honey-blond hair. "Pleased to meet you," he said with a firm handshake. He led me into a tidy office and asked to see my photos. I handed over some shots I'd had my roommate take in which I leaned against a gold pedestal in front of a draped, blood-red curtain. (In retrospect that does seem a bit overwrought. Perhaps the Caligula comparison had gone to my head.)

After examining the photos, Mr. Agent addressed me haltingly. "Frankly, they look a bit, well, *arty*. I need men who are *proud* and *masculine*." He offered to give me a chance, on two conditions. First, I had to cut my new wave hairdo, a wild mop of curls, and second I'd need to lose some weight. Though I'd just been tactfully called a fat femme, I ignored my plummeting self-esteem and promised to drop a few pounds and visit a barber. I was actually rather lucky he didn't turn me down flat since the porn industry was fast dropping boy-next-door types like me in favor of steroid-built übermenschen whose humongously beefy muscle bodies were the exact opposite of the AIDS-wasted skeletons everyone feared becoming.

As it happened, Mr. Agent was on his way to meet a producer right then and invited me along. After a short ride in his very new, very clean car, we arrived at an unprepossessing house and were greeted at the door by an unremarkable middle-aged man: Mr. Producer. Stepping inside I was deeply dismayed by the living room. Spotless and furnished in faux-colonial style, there were surveillance cameras in every corner, lending it a nightmarish, authoritarian quality. Over the mantelpiece, on which sat photos of bland white people at graduations and weddings, hung a stuffed deer's head and a pair of crossed rifles. A set of commemorative china occupied a cupboard on one wall, another was covered by bookshelves holding finely bound classics one couldn't remove because in front of them were dozens of tiny, collectable pewter cowboys and Indians arranged as if in battle. The effect was so Republican I half expected Nancy Reagan to sweep in with a tray of big, gooey chocolate chip cookies and that crazy look in her eyes.

To hide my aesthetic revulsion, I played with a yipping little terrier that ran up to greet us. Bonding with the dog, I hoped, would make me look wholesome, uncomplicated, and therefore—to the perverted eyes of the porn moguls—attractive. After introductions we sat at a low coffee table and Mr. Agent showed Mr. Producer a loose-leaf binder containing lewd photos of the models he'd signed. After a few minutes, I heard a woman's voice singing softly in Spanish. Simultaneously Mr. Agent and Mr. Producer lowered their voices. The singing grew louder and they stood up with guilty looks on their faces, grabbed the book and scurried into the kitchen. I followed just as a stout Hispanic woman wearing an apron came into the room to dust some ceramic ducks. The smut peddlers resumed their work next to the stove, quietly discussing who'd look good sodomizing whom. A moment later the women headed into the kitchen and the men bolted up, closed their binder, and scuttled, roach-like, into an adjoining laundry alcove. Again I followed.

"*¡Hola!*" said the woman from the kitchen, retrieving a can of Lemon Pledge from under the sink.

Mr. Agent and Mr. Producer waved back with bright, nervous smiles. "Hi, Esmerelda!"

As Esmerelda left, Mr. Producer explained in a whisper, "We're not out to the maid."

To my great surprise, Mr. Producer hired me for a shoot up at the Russian River in two weeks' time. Doing my best to look proud and masculine enough to deserve my five hundred dollars (half of what several other models were paid, I later learned), I dieted, got a flattop, and borrowed a plaid, flannel shirt from my roommate. If you want to know what making a porn film is like, just pick up three or four guys you've never met off the street, take them home and set up an orgy under blazing hot lights with several strangers milling around barking directions and the ground rules that everybody must keep at least one orifice filled at all times and face in the same direction.

The cutest boy at the Russian River shoot was, to my mind, the still photographer, a quiet, wispy boy with a shock of sandy-blond hair falling over one eye like Veronica Lake. He looked like someone who listened to the Cocteau Twins and adopted rescue cats. I developed a slight crush on him that quickly evaporated when, to my everlasting shame, he made me pose in a backward baseball hat with a sleeveless tee shirt emblazoned with the silhouette of the Marlboro cowboy—I who so deeply abhor sports and smoking! Fortunately, the stills were never used. I like to think it was because the Real Me shone through the butch façade, making the pictures insufficiently proud and masculine.

Postscript: Six years after our shoot, Lon Flexxx died. He was thirty years old.

Chapter 20: More Popstitutes 1987–1989

FOR OUR FOURTH GIG, THE POPSTITUTES played a Tupperware Party (or, to be precise, *after* a Tupperware Party) held in my living room. Despite the fact that many of her potential customers sported hair colors and genders not found in nature, Vicki, our Tupperware Lady, maintained an air of imperturbable optimism and good cheer while giving her presentation. These simple plastic containers would revolutionize our kitchens, allowing us to save food *and* money while brightening our lives with cheerful colors! After her pitch, she took out a pad of order forms and asked who wanted what. The two-dozen no-goodniks who'd assembled to see our show just sat staring blankly like fidgety kids at a particularly un-fun school assembly. One girl finally bought some measuring spoons and I purchased a set of sandwich containers, but it was a plain fact we'd wasted Vicki's time in a shockingly cavalier fashion. Oh, how guilty I felt!

For our fifth gig, Diet booked us at "Club Häagen-Dazs," an ice cream parlor on Castro Street where a couple of scoopers—unbeknownst to their manager—were running an underground nightclub. The show was right before Christmas and for a finale we performed "Dance of the Sugar Plum Fairies" during which we sprinkled ourselves with powdered sugar. Apparently, the sugar fell in-between the floorboards and couldn't be vacuumed or swept up leading to a massive invasion of ants and the firing of our pals, the scoopers. *Oops!*

After that fabulous fiasco, Diet began working with a reclusive musical genius going by the name of Mudhead X. After weeks of toying and tinkering, our backing tapes' tinny, abrasive quality gave way to a bubbly danceability.

"I think we're ready for the big time!" Diet exulted.

"Meaning what?" I asked.

"We'll play in clubs and get paid!"

"Great!"

"And we need more people so we can really give 'em the ol' razzle dazzle."

Throughout 1987 and '88, Diet added ever more band members to play gigs he booked at a series of tiny venues. Along with dozens of club kid special guest stars who joined us on an intermittent basis, like Jupiter and Quartknee, he recruited three new permanent full-time Popstitutes: Fruit Fly, a self-professed fag hag, who ran around in a French maid's uniform with fly wings sermonizing about something she called "porno-logic;" Zeon, an actual teenager who rapped about growing up gay in San Francisco; and Tyler-Bob, an art student with an unnatural fondness for glitter.

These added Popstitutes were needed because Diet had decided all our songs should be acted out in neo-vaudevillian synchronized dance review style—like something from *The Carol Burnett Show* or a Mitzi Gaynor TV special. Suddenly we needed different sets, props, and costumes for every song! This was hard enough when we did forty-minute sets, but Diet was also fond of medleys. In the space of fifteen minutes one might be expected to change from a space outfit constructed from Mylar and hula-hoops into a green satin choir robe (culled from the trash) then strip to leopard print bikini briefs, then don a cowboy hat and a stuffed animal horse turned into a tutu, all while doing very specific choreography and singing back-up. Everyone pleaded with him to simplify, but when challenged Diet turned into a shrill, *my-way-or-the-highway* despot. All he needed was a monocle, jodhpurs, and a riding crop. What made his dramatic ambitions especially deluded was that we only held one rehearsal before each gig and everyone invariably showed up late and loaded. Diet would be pontificating about, say, the best way to make a posé turn while wearing a giant, furry mouse outfit while all around him everyone was drinking, gossiping, and doing lines.

Our complete lack of theatrical professionalism turned what could have been a terpsichorean tornado of radical homo hotness into a loosey-goosey art-for-art's-sake Dionysian free-for-all. Performances were plagued by technical difficulties, missed cues, and lost props. Yet even on those rare occasions when we approximated Diet's grandiose vision, I suspect audiences were mystified by all the chaos. Some people professed to like us, and I imagine there *could be* something interesting about bunch of nubile young freaks writhing around clad in day-glow body paint, fake fur, fetish-wear, and glitter. Still, our messiness frustrated me.

The one part of the Popstitutes I liked was creating posters, flyers, and show programs. These were low-tech concoctions produced with rub-on lettering from the art supply store and smutty, funny, or disturbing images cut from old magazines. It was time consuming, but fun. That job also saved me from helping Tyler and Brad with more tedious tasks like painting the easy-to-assemble *(not!)* go-go cage, glitterizing platform boots, or helping Diet with his increasingly baroque multi-colored hairdos. How baroque? Think of those stripe-y, zig-zag Ukrainian Easter eggs. *That* baroque.

The public's reaction to us was decidedly mixed. Sometimes gay audiences assumed we were sloppy drag queens (wrong—we were neither expressing nor satirizing femininity), but usually they found us amusing. Straight audiences, on the other hand, were often offended. When we played fancy-schmancy Club DV8 the management cut our set short and took our names off the marquee before we'd made it out of the building. Some punks objected to us on the grounds that synthesized music was commercial and inauthentic. Diet would gleefully argue back that guitars were phallic symbols and thus tools of patriarchy, and anyway, being anti-commercial was elitist. Regular rocker dudes would just call us fags and threaten to punch our faces, which we thought was great. We wanted them to come out of the closet with their intolerance and look ridiculous for being offended by our cartoonish homoeroticism.

Except—actually—I was offended too . . . or at least embarrassed. Brad, for reasons I didn't care to contemplate, had grown obsessed with producing prop penises. First, he made an oversized male unit out of papier-mâché into which he inserted a can of aerosol whip cream. During each show he'd pull this out and spray the audience, a great crowd pleaser. Then he concocted an eight-foot-high dancing wiener, followed by one constructed along the lines of a Chinese New Year's parade dragon, after which three cardboard guitars that flipped over and became—you guessed it. I tried to convince myself these props were necessary provocations against sexual repression in general and the demonization of gay sex in particular but couldn't. I found them vulgar and unseemly.

"Tell Brad to cut it out," I pleaded to Diet. "We're becoming X-rated buffoons!"

He scowled. "Don't be such a prude."

"I'm not!" I protested. "Tyler's dick thing-y doesn't bother me." Tyler-Bob had made a gold lamé penis emblazoned with the Macy's logo that ejaculated play money to critique the conflation of sex and social status, which I thought wittily poignant.

"You just like Tyler's 'cause it doesn't look real," said Diet.

"Well, so what if I am a prude." I countered. "Is that a crime?"

"Just the other night you were going on about Wilhelm Reich's theory that sexual repression is key to forming authoritarian personality structures."

"But I said it was probably wrong! The ancient Romans weren't sexually repressed and they were total authoritarians!"

Diet spoke soothingly. "People *like* penises. They're funny."

"Sex is sexier when it's shrouded in mystery!" I countered.

Diet chortled meanly. "Says a man who works in the nude."

"That's different!"

"Why?"

"Because *I'm quitting the band* is why!"

"Fine," said Diet, icy as a Sno-Kone. "I'm tired of being friends with you anyway."

Diet's eyebrows were telegraphing pure wrath, but I didn't believe he'd really drop me as a friend. Still, I could easily imagine him cold-shouldering me for a long, long while. Allowing such a thing was unthinkable as hanging out with Diet constituted 90 percent of my social life. I backed down.

Besides, performing with the group *could* still be interesting. Among Diet's innumerable pet peeves was the new trend of Karaoke. "People should write their own songs, not ape corporate approved celebrities!" he declared. Never one to disapprove in silence, he brought The Popstitutes to a White Horse Karaoke night on his thirtieth birthday and signed up to sing. After an eternity of guys belting out Barbra or wailing like Whitney, the MC finally called on us.

"Now it's time for the . . . what is this? Popstitooties?"

We all followed Diet as he bounded up to the mic. "It's Popstitutes. And we've changed our mind about what to sing. Play this." He handed the MC one of his own tapes. "It's all cued up and ready to go." The MC shrugged and did as he was told. Strange noise-music blared (imagine a steam locomotive crossed with a printing press) as Diet began chanting: "Turning thirty! This is not Iran! Strip!" We all stripped to our skivvies and danced about madly while Diet, for extra percussion, spanked Zeon's naked posterior. When our brief interruption of the corporate monoculture ended, half the audience stood frozen and half clapped weakly as we bowed and left the stage to reward ourselves with too many cocktails.

The Popstitutes plugged along doing a show every few months up into the early '90s when Diet became otherwise occupied and allowed the band to fade into the mists of entertainment oblivion. When it was finally over, I felt sort of relieved. We'd never made money, gotten *way* fewer groupies than planned, and our one shot at recording a single had gone awry when Diet and the producer argued so much, they stopped speaking. People have told me they found us inspiring, which I take to mean our ostentatious rejection of prissiness and passivity made them feel less alone in choosing to be loudmouth freakazoids. And I like to think that The Popstitutes, along with all the other obscure queer performance artists, did produce at least some resistance to the normalizing tide. I'm not sure how much actual dissent we inspired, but our failure to rally the masses hardly mattered. In the years since the band started, the vibe in gaydom switched decisively—all on its own—from demoralized passivity to boiling outrage.

Chapter 21: The Boiling Outrage

THE ACT UP DEMO WAS VERY much like every other demo. We stood, listened to speeches, clapped, chanted, waved signs, listened to more speeches, clapped more, chanted more, on and on. Diet and I found such predictability unscintillating, but suffered through it gladly because the issues were so very life-and-death: the FDA's slowness in approving AIDS drugs, the illegality of needle exchange programs, the prioritizing of military boondoggles over public healthcare. The government was acting as if an effective, compassionate response to the plague would give it Gay Cooties. Many of us at the rally wore safety whistles on lanyards around our necks (to be blown in case of queer bashing), and at the crescendo of the keynote speech we used them to add an ear-deafening *screeeee!* to the clapping, whooping, and chanting. The police encircling us took this as the cue to terminate the protest with their usual street-clearing lockstep maneuver. Diet and I slipped away before they reached our end of the crowd, not wanting to join the legions of activists (and bystanders) who'd been viciously clubbed or stomped.

Many, if not most, of the protesters belonged to a new breed: the professional AIDS Activist, instantly recognizable because of their amazing fashion sense: tight jeans, message tee shirts, black Doc Marten boots, and black leather motorcycle jackets covered in stickers bearing slogans in no-nonsense *sans serif* lettering SILENCE = DEATH! FIGHT AIDS, NOT PEOPLE WITH AIDS! MEN, USE CONDOMS OR BEAT IT! The activists' clone-ish uniformity could have been off-putting but it was for a worthy cause, so it wasn't. For reasons unknown, the *most* beautiful boys became the *most* committed activists and the demos got a reputation as good cruising spots. I never got lucky at one, but Diet and I attended all the big rallies because to stand amidst a sea of sexy, outraged activists felt like spitting in the very face of death itself.

Attending rallies was not considered "enough" by activists; responding to an existential threat required getting arrested and attending meetings. I avoided arrest because people in uniforms terrify me, but I did try a couple of meetings. Scores of activists, faces shining with nobility of purpose, sat on folding chairs in the assembly room of The Women's Building. They discussed goals and strategies with such formidable intelligence, intensity, and acrimony, I concluded there was nothing a goofball like me could contribute. My support for The Struggle would consist of attending rallies and offering my lovin' to as many activists as would have me. Every tryst with one of these danger-defying heroes felt romantically virtuous, like a WWII-era English lass giving herself to a brave RAF pilot. *Swoon!*

Queer Nation formed to deal with the homophobia that underlay the government's non-response to AIDS, the uptick in anti-gay street violence, and the never-ending drone of homophobic slurs excreting from the mouths of politicians, religious leaders, and celebrities. Some gay squares couldn't grasp the concept of re-appropriating the epithet "queer" and wrote weepy/angry letters-to-the-editor lamenting the organization's name. This might have inspired sympathy rather than hilarity were the same squares not simultaneously attacking Queer Nation for "outing" closet case gays who hypocritically supported anti-gay bigotry. Along with the obligatory street protests, posters, and stickers—QUEERS BASH BACK! DYKE POWER! INCITE QUEERNESS!—Queer Nation increased visibility with "kiss-ins" at bars, restaurants, and malls. I attended one at a suburban shopping plaza where after kissing our same-sex comrades we all kissed someone wearing a giant Hello Kitty costume outside the Sanrio store, inadvertently foreshadowing the inclusion of "plushies" in our rainbow of delightful deviance.

Also in the name of visibility, *activiste extraordinaire* Ggreg Taylor rented one of the Green Tortoise "hippie" buses, redubbed it "the Lavender Tortoise," and took thirty-seven of his nearest and dearest friends, including The Popstitutes, to Disneyland. Chanting, "We're here! We're queer! Get used to it!" or, "Two, four, six, eight! How do you know your kids are straight?" would've gotten us disappeared into Disneyland's legendary underground dungeon in microseconds, so we opted for the Liberace strategy of flaunting our queerness solely through fashion and flounce. Thus, after a long ride and a night of partying in a sleazy motel, we all turned up at the gates of the Magic Kingdom dressed to dazzle in muumuus, Mardi Gras beads, cha-cha heels, unitards, *whatever.*

Disney security denied us entrance at first, but eventually agreed to let us in if they could search us. What they expected to find, I can't imagine, but the rather nellie guard who riffled my bag whispered, "It's shameful the way they're treating you!" Once inside we proceeded to spend the day enjoying rides and perplexing small children who couldn't figure out which fairytale we belonged in.

Ggreg Taylor also lurked behind the founding of Boy with Arms Akimbo, a DIY cultural activist group responsible for "graphic interventions," late night campaigns that covered the city with posters combining naughty pictures and the slogan, "Sex Is." In a nation experiencing a backlash against the Sexual Revolution, this qualified as a bold political statement. Just then, the city was covered in queer activist posters. One, wheat-pasted to a highway pillar near my home, read ACT UP, FIGHT BACK! and featured a two-foot high cartoon head with spike-y hair screaming maniacally, as if locked in battle with an army of Hell Beasts, or perhaps FDA bureaucrats. Then there were the "Read My Lips" posters showing either a pair of cute sailor boys or of hot lesbians kissing, a cheery sight in a world where positive images of same-sex lovin' were rare. Some posters listed the crimes of anti-gay bigots like Jesse Helms, Cardinal O'Connor, and President Bush (*père*), along with hideously unflattering portraits of the same. These functioned both as straight (you should pardon the expression) propaganda *and* turf markers, announcing that the street on which they appeared was queer-friendly, or at least contested territory.

Imagine, then, how my friends and I felt when a group of Castro merchants formed The Golden Broom, an organization dedicated to eradicating what they saw as the urban blight of posters! It appalled us that anyone would value mere tidiness over free speech, especially gay people whose very survival depended on activism.

A heartening side effect of the activist upsurge was a truce between gay men and lesbians. Overnight, the instinctive animosity of yesteryear became passé. The cynical view is that the men were too busy with the plague to hog the movement all to themselves, but I never entirely bought that. The activist guys I knew seemed truly interested in working with gals; and the gals were not only happy to pitch in politically, great numbers became volunteer caregivers for people with AIDS.

Being supporters of The Struggle, The Popstitutes were occasionally incorporated into demonstrations.

Example #1: Picture me writhing on the sidewalk outside Macy's Union Square on Black Friday while someone dressed as a can of Coors beer pretend-kicks me and someone dressed as a pack of Marlboros pretend-clubs me with a giant cigarette. Diet sings "The Mugging" and earnest young activists hand out flyers urging a boycott of Coors and Marlboro for funding anti-gay politicians. Pedestrians ignore us as they rush by in search of gifts.

Example #2: An evangelical preacher in the Sunset District publicly urged that gays be put to death, so The Popstitutes joined the Sisters of Perpetual Indulgence for a counter-sermon. I brought along the day-glow orange cross on which I, dressed as a playboy bunny, had been crucified at a gig the preceding Easter and we produced some convoluted street theater. Theater is the only weapon available to the penniless and powerless, so we were doing the best we could but—alas—our little show was both inaudible and invisible to the congregants inside the church, which resembled nothing so much as a WWII bunker with stained glass windows and a spire that could've functioned as a gun turret.

Diet and I never discussed it, but we both knew the giant corporations and religious zealots we were protesting barely noticed our existence. Such bogeymen lived in "the real world," a place where the theatrically-expressed opinions of oddly-dressed youngsters meant less than nothing. That our demonstrations didn't change a lot of minds didn't make them entirely useless, though. Sometimes you have to preach to the choir to make them sing louder. Plus, our ineffectual protests made us feel better, like kicking a cabinet door on which you've banged your shin. And maybe, just maybe, by registering our objection to being reviled we salvaged a bit of dignity. Whatever the case, protesting kept us busy—essential since we were young and incapable of sitting still.

Chapter 22: Clubs, Queens, Scenes, and Zines

FOR YEARS AFTER AIDS STARTED GRABBING headlines, a miasmic gloom hung over gay San Francisco. Bars and clubs sat half empty because people were afraid of catching the virus from cocktail glasses, or demoralized by the newly ascendant anti-gay bigotry, or ashamed the illness had robbed them of their beauty, or scared by the new spate of queer bashings, or just busy navigating medical mazes and minefields.

The news HIV wasn't transmitted casually and the sight of AIDS activists taking on the plague shifted the mood decisively. Suddenly, people wanted to kick up their heels and be around others enduring the same traumas. Nightlife didn't quite regain the manic intensity of the pre-AIDS era, but by the late '80s, once-a-week clubs devoted to particular varieties of music (Techno-Acid-Trip House or Industrial-Breakbeat or Ambient-Jungle-Dub or what have you) began popping up around town like mushrooms after a summer rain. Often found in the diviest of dive bars, they generally had provocative names like Fag Club, Chaos, or Faster Pussycat, and were *incredibly* fun.

Among the most ardent club-hoppers were a number of gender-ambivalent types we called "queens." Some were straight up dragsters, but others were people (of various sexes) who, in the process of becoming nightclub personalities, had somehow completely thrown off the shackles of the binary gender system. Prone to dancing on tables, alcoholic excess, and zany antics, the queens acted as cheerleaders for vivacity, their eccentricities and flamboyance making everyone feel a little braver and freer. Death lost some of its terror in the face of someone like "Hannah Barbaric" dressed as a slatternly cave woman wearing a ragged leopard print frock and a bone in her hair like Pebbles Flintstone. Not only did queens enjoy the status of beloved entertainers, everyone respected their death-defying bravery in parading their queerness on public streets.

It bothered me slightly that a lot of queens were prone to making a big show of groping the butchest of butch guys. In doing so they simultaneously reversed the traditional gender dynamic, which I thought ok, but also reinforced it by exalting butchness as the pinnacle of desirability. Complicated! Gender theory was only just then becoming a hot topic in academia, but the queens already had a lot of ideas. You might hear assertions that there were actually 247 distinct sexes or that one could alter one's gender along a spectrum depending on mood. "Oh, I'm feeling sixty-forty today, advantage *male*." I don't know if our little scene would qualify as enlightened by modern standards, but the prevailing attitude in alterna-queer clubland was *who cares what gender anyone is, so long as they look faaabulous!*

I marveled at the planning Miss Kitty Litter Green put into her performance of "Doll on A Music Box," a song from the wonderfully horrible 1968 children's film, *Chitty Chitty Bang Bang*. Dressed as the female lead, Truly Scrumptious, who in turn was dressed as a wind-up Bavarian Maiden doll, Kitty did a flawlessly mechanical dance while slowly rotating on a platform. Half parody, half heartfelt homage, her performance perfectly expressed the ambivalence we all felt toward Hollywood schmaltz: People who rejected schmaltz completely were humorless Stalinists who only appreciated art as political propaganda while those who embraced it uncritically (or unironically) were insufferably insipid. After Kitty got *sick* she became obsessed with healing green energy supposedly being beamed at her from outer space. A beautifully loopy idea.

The Sluts A-Go-Go drag troupe worked an ultra-garish 1960s aesthetics: high, high heels; big, big wigs; truckloads of jewelry; and enough make-up for a brothel-full of tarts. They favored eye-blindingly day-glow colors and painted their teeth pure white so that their smiles were positively alarming. They were always holding cocktail parties, hitting the clubs dressed to the nines, and putting on variety shows full of clever skits (like a fight scene from *Who's Afraid of Virginia Woolf* in which the shrewish Martha has two heads). They even staged a couple of full-length plays: *The Bad Seed*, a 1950s psychodrama about a sweet little girl who's secretly a murderous psychopath, and the aforementioned version of Genet's *The Balcony*.

The Sluts' leader was Doris Fish, née Philip Mills, a handsome, square-jawed Australian with an accent so crisp and bracing it felt like a slap of aftershave. He started performing in Sydney with a political drag troupe, Sylvia and the Synthetics, then came to SF and hooked up with Miss X and Tippi at a come-as-your-favorite-Fellini-character party (doesn't that sound fun?). Miss X worked a severe, waspish look described as "1930s predatory lesbian." A wry, dry wit, Miss X sang her own smutty version of Cole Porter's "You're the Top" and always played the tough, exasperated Joan Crawford-types in productions. Tippi was billed as "the world's oldest living child star in captivity" and did seem extremely childlike, if you can imagine a perversely naughty child with a strong penchant for vodka. I once ran across her in the toy section of the downtown Woolworth's staring longingly at Nastina, a green-skinned doll, half witch, half spider. "I want it but I can't afford it," she explained pitifully.

The whole town knew the Sluts, along with their dashing young director/producer, Phillip R. Ford, were filming a feature length movie: *Vegas in Space*, a drag-tacular sci-fi spoof set on an "all female pleasure planet." The production was funded by Doris's work as a male escort and whatever the cast and crew could scrounge up, which wasn't much. The low budget led to all manner of clever innovations, like the extraterrestrial city constructed from lipsticks and perfume bottles. That ordinary San Francisco deviants were self-producing a feature length film gave one the feeling anything was possible. Like Peter Pan, with faith, and trust, and a little fairy dust (or if that was in short supply, amphetamines) we could fly, we could fly, *we could fly*!

In 1991, after almost a decade of nearly round-the-clock work, *Vegas in Space* held its grand opening at the Castro Theater. The venerable movie palace was lit with klieg lights and the whole of hip San Francisco turned out dressed in their glamtastic best to sip champagne and hail the creation of a new masterpiece. Only Doris and Tippi didn't make it, each having died just a few weeks previously. I was invited to Doris's memorial but didn't attend because I was going into plague denial, thinking *this is not happening, this is not happening, this is not happening.* I was somehow calm enough to attend Tippi's, but I kept expecting her to walk into the room at any minute. A different type of denial.

San Francisco is a world-class Freak Magnet, but even here Jerome Caja stood out. He clothed his anemically scrawny body in skimpy outfits composed of torn fishnets, hideous floral negligees, saran wrap, dime-store bangles, and gutter trash. Stringy hair, smudgy make-up, and a never-ending string of insane facial expressions completed the look. This might sound like scare-queen drag, but Jerome actually looked quite beautiful, like an Egon Schiele painting come to life. This was no accident. Jerome was a fine artist of growing repute who used nail polish to create irreverent, funny, perverse, disturbing little paintings, often involving clowns, priests, and eggs. When Jerome died, alterna-queer San Francisco became like a jigsaw puzzle missing a piece right in the middle.

Except that the alterna-queer city of the late '80s and early '90s actually had no middle. It was a series of overlapping, amorphous groups comprised of people who shared nothing more than an aptitude for activism, a penchant for perversion, and a fetish for flamboyance. There were distinct queer contingents within every major sub-cultural tendency—spoken word artists, underground filmmakers, indie rockers, neo-pagans, and a whole ton more. Each of these groups provided an alternative to the gay mainstream while promoting queer visibility to their straight counterparts.

Modern primitives were one of the newest and most visible additions to the subcultural panoply. Their fashion consisted of activist or punk drag plus extreme body modification, which could consist of anything from earlobe-extensions to tribal tattoos to branding to scarification to multiple piercings of ear, nose, lip, neck, nipple, and a region I shan't name but the piercing of which is called a "Prince Albert." Along with manly pursuits like S&M, riding motorcycles, or ritualistic drumming, queer "mod prims" enjoyed dancing at clubs with names like Screw and Fiend. The industrial music they liked was too self-serious about being edgy and aggro for my taste, but I often endured it because the boys were invariably sizzling-hot.

Also prone to sizzling-hotness, queer punks were suddenly everywhere. They had their own bands like the Comrades in Arms and Tribe 8, the exploits of which were detailed in the local zine, *Homocore*, put out by Deke Nihilson and Tom Jennings. They frequently lived in squats or warehouse collectives with names like Shred of Dignity (which had the fabulous address of 666 Illinois Street) and went in for all manner of anarchist agitation. In 1989, queer punks joined forces with Club Chaos and The Popstitutes to enter a float in the pride parade. We all felt the boring business-sponsored floats and politicians waving from convertibles were missing the spirit of a day meant to commemorate the Stonewall riots. To make our point we had our own contingent: all the wildest queer kids in town dancing on top of a smashed-up cop car (well, it was painted like a cop car) that was being crushed by a gigantic papier-mâché high-heeled pump. Legend has it we neglected to pay our fees or even register and actually had to crash the parade.

Anarchic in a different way were the local club kids. Like their more-famous New York cousins, who were always appearing on daytime talk shows, their claim to fame was a dedication to brain-scramblingly outré outfits. Dressed as human candelabras, monster clowns, extra-terrestrial hookers, or what have you, they provoked wonderment in all who saw them. Diet and I approved of them because in hitting town without trying to look sexy or rich we thought they were subtly critiquing conformism and social climbing. The political ramifications of this critique were slight, though, as the club kids mostly wound up functioning as party mascots for the rave scene. Ravers were kids who lived to dance in gigantic crowds of kids dancing. Like their disco forbearers, ravers embraced a blandly universalist *music brings people together* ethos that precluded homophobia, but didn't advocate for anything more than having a good time, ie. getting looped and dancing to acid house while waving glow-sticks for eleventy-three hours straight.

Certain excitable subcultural theorists claimed the ravers' habit of eschewing booze in favor or ecstasy (aka MDMA) and "smart drugs" (aka herbal supplements alleged to boost intelligence) would combine with their chosen music's hypnotic beats and positive lyrics to rewire the ravers' brains. They'd become neurologically incapable of fear, greed, hate, or territoriality and usher in a high-tech, neo-tribal future wherein everyone devoted themselves to creativity and dancing. I totally supported rewiring people's brains but couldn't fully appreciate the scene because I found the music mind-numbingly repetitive.

I did, however, enjoy the club kid-sponsored rave-style Outlaw Parties, zany affairs during which gaggles of youngsters would invade some public place (a BART train, say, or the asphalt nowhere-land under a freeway) and throw a shindig using a portable sound system. Transforming spaces of glum functionality into zones of bubbling frivolity felt liberating and reminded me of old movies in which tipsy revelers conga lined out of their party and through the streets. Also in their favor, Outlaw Parties never went on too long because the police invariably showed up to disperse everyone before things got dull. Surprisingly, they always did this with good cheer, a real contrast to Castro Halloween parties, which always ended with riot cops marching down the street violently smashing their batons against their shields.

Uranus took place Sunday nights at The End Up, a space reputedly haunted by the ghost of a former owner allegedly buried beneath the flagstones on the back the patio. The DJs, Mike Blue and Lewis Walden, played techno-industrial music (to this day I think of 808 State's "Cubik" every time I see them) along with a few camp oldies (like Lipps Inc.'s "Funkytown") and hired the sexiest boys and craziest queens in town (including, occasionally, me and a few other Popstitutes) to go-go dance, creating a deliciously out-of-control vibe. What really made the club legendary, though (along with lots of gay-boys gettin' lucky) was its astounding mix. Along with the usual hard-bodied hotties, pretty young twinks, and druggy dance queens, it attracted modern primitives, transfolk (all varieties), club kids, drag queens, and lesbians (all varieties). More unusual still, members of these disparate groups occasionally spoke to one another! The plague and the insurgency it fueled were forging a previously unknown camaraderie *and it was fun.*

Just then, fun was a political issue. For decades the media had painted gay men as sad victims of loneliness, depression, suicide, insanity, and/or murder. The *Gay=Tragic* meme receded a bit during the height of '70s hedonism, but was making a strong '80s comeback with the modern twist that our inevitable bad end now came from AIDS. The new innocent victim gayboys might be sympathetic, but the pity they evoked felt maudlin and slightly toxic. People wanted to end their days in a party, not a puddle of tears.

Another spot where all of queerdom converged was Café Flore, a woodsy Castro corner café with big windows and an outdoor patio. Always packed with activists, club promoters, writers, artistes, photographers, performers, drag queens, and scene-makers, it functioned as a sort of perpetual cocktail party and primitive internet. One could hear all the best gossip and buzz just by tablehopping. Up the street were several new and used record stores, including specialty shops where DJs went in search of the latest hard-to-find import maxi-singles. Finally, near the corner of Castro sat the copy shop where everyone photocopied the posters and flyers advertising the endless stream of actions and events.

The copy shop was also full of people producing queer zines, the small circulation magazines that'd become popular with the advent of punk's DIY ethos and cheap photocopying. Anyone with something to say and a few dollars could churn them out to give or sell to friends and curious strangers. A few, like *Diseased Pariah News*, *Holy Titclamps*, and *My Comrade*, grew popular enough that record stores and bookshops carried them. Enthralled by the cavalcade of verbiage and eager to join the fun, I began penning wry little essays and joined forces with fellow Popstitute Tyler-Bob to put out three issues of *Tantrum*. We got them in stores, sold copies from a card table at Uranus, and even went all the way to Los Angeles for Spew 2, the second of three queer zine conventions, to confabulate with our fellow litterateurs.

Putting out zines was the first creative activity I'd undertaken without Diet, and it gave me a new sense of myself. I wasn't just a sidekick, but a member of that strange and wondrous tribe: queer writers. Such creatures were known for their blistering wit, keen insight, and dissolute personal habits. I had the last of these down, I just needed to work on the first two. Once I'd made it (how long would it take? A year? Two?) I'd be feted and fawned over by people of substance at literary salons and cocktail parties. I could hardly wait!

The mad swirl of radical queer activism and cultural ferment swept through America's gay ghettoes like a twister. Or was it more like a crusade? How about a whirlwind with a very strong agenda? Oh, let's just say twister. Could it sweep away the complacency and self-loathing that made us vulnerable to, and occasionally complicit with, the larger society's murderous homophobia? I rather thought, yes. It was a pretty big twister. Would it be enough to save us from the plague? There I was less sure. Only medical science cures diseases. Sometimes I'd think, "They can't cure ALS. They can't cure cancer. They can't cure the common cold. None of this will make a lick of difference if they can't cure AIDS."

Chapter 23: The Test, 1989

ONE DAY I WAS WHINING so piteously and tediously about the difficulty of finding a boyfriend that my adorable, sprite-like pal, Bobby Wonders, offered help. "I know what you should do," he said, his big, elfin eyes twinkling with mischief. "Come with me to Botanica Yoruba."

"Botana whah?" I asked.

"Botanica Yoruba," repeated Bobby. "It's a Santeria shop."

"What's Santeria?" I asked.

"It's like a Caribbean folk religion," Bobby explained. "Kind of a cross between Voodoo and Catholicism. Just come along and see. You'll love it." Bobby's impish dimples left me no choice but to obey. We bussed from his Bernal Heights flat down to 22nd and Mission where we quickly found the Botanica nestled between a shop selling irregular socks and a Mexican produce market. As we pushed through the glass door to go inside, the noisy, bustling Barrio-vibe of Mission Street gave way to an otherworldly stillness and quiet. The air inside was smoky with a strange, vaguely tropical incense. Behind a low glass counter in the back sat a wizened, elderly woman of Afro-Caribbean ethnicity wearing a short white turban, all-white clothes, and an expression of timeless sagacity. She acknowledged our entrance with a tiny nod, but otherwise remained unnaturally motionless, staring straight ahead as if entranced by a mystic apparition.

The wall to my right was lined floor to ceiling with plaster saint statuettes, necklaces made from beads and shells, and incense sticks, along with bottles of magical unguents, magical potions, magical soaps, and magical floor wax. The wall to my left was devoted to colored candles in ten-inch high round glass cases imprinted with incantations, prayers, and images. Some images were recognizably Catholic like the Infant of Prague or St. John the Conqueror, but who were Chango, Oshun, and Elegua? Noting my perplexity, Bobby whispered, "Those are the Santeria gods, the Orishas, borrowed from the Yoruba religion of West Africa." I also saw candles displaying neither saints nor gods, but instead focusing on specific needs or desires: Fast Money, Un-Crossing (whatever that was), Law Stay Away, and Attraction. "See," Bobby whispered again, pointing to the attraction candles. "You can order up a boyfriend with voodoo."

"But they're so heterosexual," I complained. The Attraction candles all depicted conjoined male and female symbols.

"Not this one." Bobby held up a "Heart's Desire" candle that was imageless, but provided a blank space for writing one's wish on the glass casing.

Figuring "what the heck," I shelled out three dollars and took it home. That night I wrote "a boy" on the blank space, lit the candle, and dutifully recited the prayer printed on the side of the glass. As a confirmed agnostic, I did this in the spirit of a lark, but allowed myself to feel a tiny bit hopeful just for fun. Following the candle's instructions, I repeated the prayer every morning on waking and every night before falling asleep. A week later the very last bit of wax burned away, but somehow, the tiny orange flame on the remnant of wick at the bottom kept burning. Logic and science dictated the tiny flame should die, yet it burned *on and on and on* with no source of energy *for three miraculous days*. On the evening of that third day, exactly at sunset, the flame flared, sputtered loudly, and then extinguished itself in a puff of smoke just as the glass casing shattered with a loud *scrack!*

Agnostic or not, I knew an omen when I saw one. I put on my sexiest outfit—torn jeans over paisley pajama bottoms, two studded leather belts, black Doc Martens, multiple plastic beaded necklaces, and a sleeveless tee shirt emblazoned with the image of Andy Warhol and a soup can—and went dancing at The Stud. At first nothing seemed enchanted—just another night of youngsters shaking their booties to New Order and the Cure. Then I saw Him. Lurking impudently in a corner stood a rail thin boy in a black trench coat with spiky Sid Vicious hair and the face of a wayward angel. He noticed me too, we said hello, and together we danced a dance as old as time. Heading back to my place the boy pulled me by the hand into every alleyway so we could kiss and kiss and kiss. The night proved a romantical success and we began dating.

Unsurprisingly for someone conjured by Voodoo, Tony Vaguely proved a rather spooky character. He burned Tibetan incense, read tarot cards, and could talk to animals. This last point may sound dubious, but I saw squirrels come up to him and chitter away as if conversing with Dr. Doolittle himself. Fashion-wise, Tony worked a sort of groovy-ghoulie punk look, pairing studded leather and black denim with polyester photo-print disco shirts, vampire hunter capes, and psychedelic purple sunglasses. I found *everything* about Tony *très* cute, including his backstory: He'd grown up in Las Vegas (a fourth-grade field trip involved seeing Wayne Newton at a casino), but spent his teen years on a hippie goat farm in Arizona. After dropping out of high school he ran off to Flagstaff where he washed dishes and played in a couple of bands: the Roto-Rooters and the Maude Squad (that name involves a fiendishly clever pun only apparent to those with a working knowledge of 1970s TV). He'd been on his way to Seattle to join friends when I waylaid him with my candle magic.

Tony was eager to escape the grubby SRO hotel where he was staying, and I was feeling impetuous (as per usual), so after a week of nonstop dating we decided he should move in with me. I was still living in the tiny crowded flat on Moss Street with Diet and a few other miscreants and my room barely outsized an elevator, but lovebirds aren't bothered by such trifles. Tony settled right in and happiness reigned. Diet usually ignored my paramours, but with Tony living under his roof it wasn't long before he tried one of his "the trouble with you is . . ." rants. I would've sprung to Tony's defense, but it proved unnecessary. Diet might as well have been prosecuting a cat; his words couldn't penetrate Tony's reality. Bowing to defeat, Diet recruited Tony to prance around on stage with The Popstitutes, but otherwise paid him no mind.

Tony and I were well matched in that his devotion to go-go, camp, and kitsch rivaled my own. He quickly found a job at

Community Thrift and began dragging home armloads of treasure: Hip Flip, a party game involving lurid groin swiveling, beer steins in the shape of American Colonial gentlemen's heads, ceramic rabbits, black light posters and so on. When not marveling at such finds we spent countless hours cuddled up on the sofa watching old movies. My lifelong fear of being left alone and forgotten in an empty room was eclipsed by the glittering certainty that Tony and I were crazy for each other.

Then one afternoon, on concluding a furious bout of lovemaking, I discovered the condom we'd been using was

b

r

o

k

e

n

I felt as if I were plummeting down an elevator shaft. Despite the earnest entreaties of the Stop Aids Project volunteers pamphleteering on every corner of the Castro, I'd never adopted the sensible habit of discussing the virus with my lovers. I was fairly certain that Tony, being only twenty-one, was negative, while I . . . The inescapable conclusion was so awful I hardly dared *think* it.

I'd just murdered Tony.

Seeing what must have been a horrified and horrifying look on my face, Tony sat up and saw the broken condom. "Oops," he said lightly. My guilt and terror were increased exponentially by the fact he wasn't grasping the gravity of the situation.

I wished I were dead.

I wished I'd never been born.

"I'm . . . um . . . sorry . . ."

"Have you ever been tested?" asked Tony, not sounding especially scared.

"No. I mean, why bother? What good is knowing? There's nothing they can do." We'd all heard tell of a new treatment called AZT, but word on the street was it didn't work.

"Maybe you're OK," said Tony, more hopeful than he had any right to be.

"It's . . . it's . . ." *How to put it diplomatically?* "Not likely."

"But you don't know *for sure* you're positive?"

I couldn't speak so I shook my head no.

"Well, will you find out?"

The test *terrified* me. Though certain I was positive, my unconscious irrationally believed I wouldn't get *sick* so long as this remained unconfirmed. And yet, Tony deserved to know. "OK. I'll get tested tomorrow."

For the next few hours I sat alone, wallowing in morbid self-recrimination. There was no way to know if this was an accident (defective condom) or involuntary manslaughter (I put it on wrong), but in not choosing celibacy I'd endangered a human life. Society forgave people who killed by accident while driving, but driving was an all-American activity sanctified by economic necessity, normality, and advertising. Homosexual fornication wore no such halo. Anti-gay bigots were loudly proclaiming homosexuality was inherently lethal, Safe Sex was a sham, and condoms broke all the time. Had I just proved them right?

Aside from my guilt, there were practical matters to consider. Honor decreed that if someone you were dating seriously got *sick* you couldn't just dump him, you had to stick around providing emotional, physical, and maybe even financial support. This was a heavy responsibility, albeit seldom a lengthy one since most everyone died quickly after becoming symptomatic. If I got *sick* first, I'd send Tony away so he wouldn't feel obliged to take care of me. If he got *sick* first, I'd care for him, but would he hate me? Would our friends blame me? And *ohmygod* . . . what if Tony and I both got *sick* at the same time? It was all too grotesque to contemplate.

When Diet came home, I immediately took him aside and imparted my grim news. He sat quietly for a moment, then his eyebrows lifted into arcs of compassion. "You never know. Maybe things will turn out OK. Why don't I go with you tomorrow? I might as well get tested too." He was trying to make me feel better, but it wasn't working.

The next morning, after a wretchedly sleepless night, I walked with Diet to the city-run clinic a few blocks from our flat. A proficient man drew our blood and a kindly woman gave us all sorts of pamphlets and instructions to come back in a week for our results. We walked home in silence. Gallows humor can blunt the horror of facing one's own mortality, but it's useless against guilt. The next seven days were interminable, insufferable, torturous. Over and over I'd find myself staring at Tony with pity and remorse. Every now and then he'd catch me and bark, "Cut it out!" I wished I could believe in a deity capable of altering fate and forgiving sins, but I didn't even believe in magic candles.

When the appointed day finally arrived, Diet and I marched down to the clinic with the humbled fatalism of aristocrats stepping up to the guillotine. We gave the receptionist our names and were instructed to wait. As we sat silently on the hard plastic chairs in the reception area, Diet's eyebrows furrowed into a Do Not Disturb sign. I was left to think back on that fateful year in New York that had surely sealed my doom. In my mind's eye I saw myself as a lusty, lovelorn boy of nineteen twirling away on a crowded dance floor to "Tainted Love" while the pulsing rhythms of the city throbbed through my tireless young body and my mind reeled with the unfathomable mystery and magic of it all. I'd been a confused, hopeful, frightened, euphoric, conniving, naïve, melancholy little mess, but for that whole glorious year I'd felt dizzyingly, dazzlingly *alive*. Now that year was boomeranging back to kill me.

"Mr. Orloff?" called the receptionist, "You can go in now." She pointed to an ominously closed door. I stood facing it, but couldn't quite force myself to use it. Diet gave me a small, forced smile of encouragement. Drawing on this, I managed to push through into a white room where a woman in a white lab-coat sat at a desk. In her hands, she held a sheet of paper on which was inscribed my fate. My psyche clenched into a tight, defensive ball as I slunk into the chair facing her. Would I get the ugly purple lesions, the bloody cough, the violent diarrhea, the rapid wasting, or all of the above? Would I go quickly or hang on for months getting sicker and sicker till I begged for death's release?

The woman looked up and smiled. "Good news, no HIV."

The air filled with confetti, bluebirds sang, and the clouds of doom parted to reveal a special ray of sunshine just for me. Tony was safe. Life would go on. I barely heard the woman as she suggested I retake the test in six months since it wouldn't show if I'd been recently infected. I'd been scrupulously safe for years, so that possibility didn't worry me. In fact, *nothing* worried me. I floated back into the waiting room and delivered the news to Diet, uttering only the single most beautiful word in the English language. "Negative."

Before he could respond, the receptionist called Diet's name. Without hesitating he strode into the office I'd just left. As I waited, my mood switched to dread. How would I go on if . . . My mind blanked, refusing to imagine the unimaginable. Diet spent far longer in the office than I had, during which time the seconds became centuries and my mood shifted to abject terror. When he finally came out, he was not smiling.

The poet Muriel Rukeyser once put it that, "The universe is made of stories, not atoms." Diet and I wouldn't have disagreed, but what we really believed was that the universe was made of jokes. Some were silly, like the infinite weirdness of babies, the double-edged sword of booze, or the brilliant stupidity of television. Others were bawdy, like the human body with its odd effluviums and glaringly obvious design flaws. Especially hilarious was the male sex organ, by turns hopeful, imperious, and needy, but always oblivious to social rectitude and its realistic chances for gratification. Many jokes were ironic, like the inability of human societies to organize humanistically, or the way people's faults are also their strengths: stubbornness doubling as perseverance, suspicion as perspicacity, or stinginess as thrift. And some jokes were just plain absurd, like how well-intentioned stupidity can inflict more suffering than intelligent malice, or the way entropy always wins in the end.

We also believed the only proper response to this universe of jokes was laughter. Not the buffoonish *har de har har* of clowns (we hated clowns), but the wry chortle and understated smirk of the wisecracking wit. Existence was hilarious and if you weren't laughing, you were *missing the point*. Serious people might find us glib, but they were just being ignorant, cowardly, dull, and stupid. *Oh, how we hated those serious people!* Well, OK, David Bowie, Patti Smith, and Martin Luther King wore it well. For most people, though, seriousness was a mistake.

This predilection for glibness was a cherished inheritance from our inverted ancestors who'd tried to snap Victorian moral crusaders out of finger-wagging mode with levity. The foremost exemplar of this pre-political survival strategy was Oscar Wilde. Diet and I both found it funny, courageous, and existentially correct that Wilde's (alleged) last words, as he lay dying in shabby hotel room, were, "Either this wallpaper goes, or I do." With that one quip, Wilde triumphed over bad interior decorating, the Victorian morality which reviled him as a sodomite, and death.

As we silently trudged home, a chill summer fog rolled in from the west, turning the blue sky a cadaverous white and leeching the city of color. I couldn't wait to give Tony the good news and I couldn't stop sneaking peeks at Diet, waiting for him to speak. When he finally did, his usual bantering tone was shot through with frustration and melancholy. "We were pioneering a new way of life with all the sex and free love, but science didn't keep up. They were too busy building bombs and sending men to the moon." His eyebrows lifted ever-so-slightly. "Clearly a case of misplaced priorities." Not hilarious, but I got the message: we were not going to become serious people.

I had to say something but wasn't up to quipping. "OK, you're infected, but you're still healthy. Maybe they'll find a cure before you even turn symptomatic."

Diet stared straight ahead. "Or, you know, maybe they won't." He turned to me his eyebrows at an accusatory slant. "You think you're negative because you were more careful than I was." His ever-loquacious eyebrows added this was evidence of playing it safe, bourgeois temperament, and weak character.

This left me momentarily speechless. Was Diet suggesting he hadn't always been completely careful? I wiped the suspicion from my mind. "I was *not* more careful. Before we knew it was sexually transmitted, I did everything everyone else did. I'm just lucky."

"And I'm not," said Diet, more to himself than me.

"Not everyone with HIV develops AIDS." I hated the hollowness of the words coming out of my mouth. "They found that one guy who's had it for, I forget, something like eight years . . ."

Diet interrupted, "You know, I'd *really* rather not talk about it anymore."

Chapter 24: Klubstitute, 1990

I WAS STANDING IN LINE TO see Pu Pu Platter who was lying nude in the fetal position on a giant bed of parsley in the middle of the dance floor. One by one the crowd of a few dozen people approached his body and squatted down for a consultation. After five minutes I finally reached Pu Pu, who I knew from outside the club as a mild-mannered, rather cerebral fellow named Steven. I knelt by his side and he handed me a small square of paper. "Here." I took my note and walked off to read it by the bar where the light was better.

"What does it say?" asked Tyler.

"Go to the restroom and use as many paper products as possible."

Tyler frowned. "That's not very environmentally conscious."

"What do you suppose it means?" I asked.

"Performance art isn't supposed to convey a specific message you can put into words," explained Tyler. "It's more supposed to raise questions or evoke feelings or de-familiarize the familiar or something."

"Huh," I said.

"Huh *indeed*," said Tyler, who could always tell when I was having a philistine reaction to art. "Well perhaps I should go get my own cryptic message." He joined the line while I signalled the bartender. Just another night at Klubstitute, *la de dah*.

* * *

IT ALL BEGAN WHEN THE SPOKEN word craze hit San Francisco. Overnight the city exploded with reading series and open mics populated by a new cohort of Beat- and punk-inspired writers. After sampling—and liking—readings at Café Babar and the Above Paradise, Diet decided to start his own queer open mic: Out of Order. It took place once a month at the Crystal Pistol, a Mission District dive bar, right before the wildly popular Club Chaos. The gimmick was that instead of a sign-up sheet, Diet randomly pulled readers' names out of a hat, ensuring nobody could wander off while waiting his or her turn to read and boorishly avoid listening to anyone else.

At some open mics I'd attended, the ratio of tedious narcissists to people with something to say and a flair for saying it reached as high as six to one. At Out of Order that ratio was reversed. Instead of whiners, ranters, Bukowski clones, and abstruse experimentalists, it attracted witty observers of the passing social scene and people addicted to self-deprecating self-revelation. People like Richard Loranger and Danielle Hell. Oh, would you like to meet Danielle? Here she comes now.

There's a smattering of applause as a young woman dressed entirely in shiny, skin-tight black PVC plastic totters up to the front of the room on stiletto-heeled boots. Her pale face is slathered in make-up and cartoonishly sexy, like a fashion illustration by Patrick Nagel. In a deep voice brimming with subtle irony she addresses the seated scenesters. "This is a poem called, *Breakfast in the Flesh District*." She holds up a sheet of notebook paper and begins to read. "The ghosts are rising over the faded marquee of a boarded-up strip club on Turk Street. Ancient girls with chipped blonde faces . . ." Everyone listens attentively and claps enthusiastically at the end. It's 1989 and sex work is a hot new topic for literary investigation. Danielle's next piece is prose, and even more popular. "When my parents weren't home I'd steal my father's *Penthouse* and masturbate to the letters in Forum, imagining that the protagonists were me and Andy Gibb, except I skipped over the oral sex because that was gross and besides, I knew that Andy Gibb would never want anything so disgusting as a blow job . . ."

Inspired by all the great writing, I began reading my personal essays at Out of Order. Although I felt nervous as a bridegroom each time, they were always well received and the applause they garnered affected me with a pink champagne giddiness. How delightful to finally discover a queer scene wherein verbal dexterity and style were valued above physical beauty and butch posturing!

Early in 1990, when Out of Order had been steadily pulling in several dozen attendees for close to a year, the Crystal Pistol's manager offered Diet Tuesday nights for a weekly club. After a quick frenzy of theorizing (during which he surely thought a lot about Club 57, stomping ground of NYC's East Village art scene, Cabaret Voltaire, birthplace of Dada, and the Kit Kat Klub from "Cabaret") he called a meeting of Popstitutes to divulge his plans. Our club, he declared loftily, wouldn't be just another hotspot for youthful gadabouts, but an incubator of imagination, a hotbed of subversion, and a haven for the misfits and mutants who move culture forward. We'd provide a venue for underexposed queer artists *and* promote cross-cultural pollination with unusual pairings: drag queens and punk bands, cabaret singers and performance art, live theater and Spoken Word. And to counteract people's lamentable tendency to slip into passive observer-dom, we'd promote audience participation by offering games, classes, contests, and crafting activities. Diet would book the acts and MC, I'd design the promo materials and DJ between acts, Tyler would work the door, and everyone would help with decoration, hostessing, and instigating a spirit of levity. Admission would be a mere ninety-eight cents, with all the money going to performers and promotion.

"Sounds amazing," I said, "but what'll we call it?"

Brad giggled. "Let's call it Klubstitute, like an institute of clubbing."

Everyone liked that idea, so that was that.

For the next few months we all went out every night to distribute flyers at bars, clubs, openings, and parties. This was exhausting, but not ruinously expensive. Diet got us in free everywhere by talking club doormen into submission (they *tried* to make us pay, but he jabbered *on and on and on* until they gave way). He was a pro at cadging free drinks as well. To me, these seemed like super-powers and I was mightily impressed. It didn't occur to me that we were actually providing free entertainment for the clubs' paying customers by showing up in kooky outfits and exuding sparkle, but I suppose we were.

Finally, Klubstitute opened. Only a few dozen people showed

up for the first night because everyone was home watching the start of the first Gulf War on TV, but we didn't give up. Week after week, month after month, we kept promoting until we'd built a loyal following of perhaps a couple hundred socially awkward malcontents and misfits with a creative bent. Now, are you ready for a night at Klubstitute? OK, let's go!

You arrive around eleven to find Tyler sitting on a bar stool outside the entrance wearing a super-funky '70s red vinyl coat, Star Wars cartoon shorts, and silver glitter knee-high boots, his green and blue hair in pink barrettes. Hand him a dollar, he hands you two cents from a plastic jack-o-lantern full of pennies. Go inside and order a cocktail from the bar on the left. There's a drink special, but no matter what they're calling it this week, it'll be a kamikaze. Make your way down a thin corridor past the pinball machines and find yourself in a low-ceilinged space not much larger than an average living room. As a few dozen mildly eccentric folks mill about expectantly, you sit at one of the three tiny tables in back and the show starts.

What will you see? Maybe Miss X singing her naughtied-up version of Cole Porter's "You're the Top." Or maybe The High Risk Group is performing a scantily clad modern dance. Or maybe Steve Abbott is reading from his novel, *The Lizard Club*. Or maybe Canadian cinematic wunderkind Bruce La Bruce is screening his fiendishly clever short films. Or maybe you'll hear some "queercore" punk bands. After the show there'll be a fun activity to finish out the night: maybe a nude sketch modeling class, or a make-over booth, or on-the-spot psychoanalysis, or palm readings, or ballroom dance lessons, or an around-the-block soapbox derby.

Diet was also terribly fond of theme nights. For Klubstihootenany everyone do-si-doed to the "dykeabilly" sound of the Bucktooth Varmits and Arturo Galster as Patsy Cline. For New Age Night people lounged inside a pretend hot tub made of cardboard and danced to whale songs. We kept the literary vibe going with Zine Nights during which the Xeroxed literati presented their wares, continued Out of Order once a month, and held a "Ho-Write" writing workshop that produced a chapbook of writings about sex work. For May Day we combined the holiday's pagan and political aspects with a pre-club protest march through the Castro behind a banner reading "No Assimilation!" followed by a traditional Maypole dance around one of Brad's six-foot high pink papier-mâché creations in the little-used public park beside the Crystal Pistol.

(The "No Assimilation!" sign, a contribution from political friends, annoyed Diet. Onlookers who weren't already steeped in radical chic orthodoxy, he pointed out, would have no clue who was not supposed to assimilate to what. Our friends had retreated so far into their bubble of like-minded leftists they'd forgotten how to communicate with average citizens. Even if people understood the message that they weren't supposed to be bourgeois or boring, why should they listen to total strangers telling them how to live? The slogan struck Diet as bossy and I had to agree.)

Hovering over the whole Klubstitute enterprise was the ghost of The Factory. Diet and I had effectively accepted Andy Warhol as our personal savior and regarded his books *Popism* and *The Philosophy of Andy Warhol* as old and new testaments. We watched Warhol films whenever screened, even the boring ones, and found his coterie of entertainingly dysfunctional superstars (apostles) endlessly fascinating. The chief precept of our Warholianism was that his notorious prediction—in the future everyone will be famous for fifteen minutes—was actually a program for redistributing fame the way socialism redistributes wealth. Dividing fame equitably would require giving the masses access to the means of cultural production, transforming them from passive consumers of corporate entertainment to empowered producers of art. It would also inspire them to forget all about the formulaic fantasies churned out by the culture industry and focus on the honest self-expression of ordinary people—leading inexorably to an upsurge in political consciousness and good taste that would sweep away celebrity gossip, the inanities of primetime TV, and perhaps capitalism itself.

I won't make grand claims, but performing at Klubstitute did sometimes transform people. Homophobia leaves many people with bad cases of self-loathing and social anxiety. A warm round of applause from peers acted as a therapeutic balm, soothing fears that one was unlikable or intrinsically inferior. Diet also had a way of intuiting when people needed prodding to display their talents.

Example #1: Diet recruited a shy lad by the name of David Hawkins to co-MC with him. Initially awkward and anxious, after few turns on the stage he blossomed into a witty and popular stand-up comedian.

Example #2: David Jude Thomas had always thought of his films as something people would only see after his death. Following the untimely demise of cinematic heart-throb River Phoenix, Diet decided the club needed some sort of tribute and produced a flyer heralding the release of *Cry Me a River*, by David Jude Thomas . . . without first asking David if he was willing to produce or screen such a film. David rose to the challenge and was blown away watching the film's emotional impact on the audience— particularly one overwrought drag queen with mascara-blackened tears running down her face as she profusely thanked him for his efforts. He began showing his films around, as well as joining the coterie of people Diet relied on for free flyer design and other favors.

Alas, unstable personalities are drawn to stages as moths to flames. For them, the spotlight at Klubstitute—like the unblinking eye of Warhol's camera—acted as a psychic X-ray machine. Under its luminescent glare they turned themselves inside out or put on masks that paradoxically revealed their innermost character. One fellow, revealing a frightful vacuity, reproduced a famous comedian's shtick, word for word, gesture for gesture. Another gave what he called a spoken word performance that consisted of hateful put-downs of various scenesters punctuated by his own braying laughter. Fortunately, such human traffic accidents were few and far between.

After a year, Klubstitute needed a larger space to accommodate larger crowds and moved to The End Up. There we held one of my favorite nights: Tippi's Prom. We slathered the space with streamers and homemade decorations so it really looked like a gussied up high school gym and everyone came dressed in their best thrift store formalwear. For entertainment we hired pint-sized powerhouse, Connie Champagne. She and her band, the Tiny Bubbles, serenaded us with contemporary hits and old standards. Like most gays I'd missed my own high school prom and wasn't prepared for the emotional impact. Slow dancing to Iggy Pop's "Shades" with Tony Vaguely wearing a tux felt totally pink cloudsville. What romance! What bliss! What magic!

* * *

IT'S A KNOWN FACT OF NIGHTLIFE that clubs need to be jam-packed or they won't seem "happening" and patrons will swarm off to more crowded spots. Every few weeks this horrid dynamic played out at Klubstitute. I'd stare at the door, waiting, waiting, waiting for people to arrive, but eventually it would be midnight and a mere two-dozen die-hards would be in attendance. Nothing is more loathsome to performers than a tiny, inattentive, and/or dwindling audience, and the mood on such nights often soured. Conversations turned to why nobody had showed up. Was it bad weather, bad promotion, bad acts, or had someone infected the club with loser cooties? Diet was the only person who truly never seemed to care about poor turnouts. He found keeping small crowds entertained an interesting challenge and never took the club's failures personally.

Diet's equanimity almost certainly derived from a moral growth spurt that occurred when he quit drinking. Apparently he'd gotten scraped off the sidewalk by police during a boozaholic blackout and spent the night in a drunk-tank. On release, he headed straight to Alcoholics Anonymous and never touched another drop. He didn't like discussing his recovery so I never learned what his Higher Power was or what he thought of the famous twelve steps . . . and it worried me. He was suddenly, for the first time ever, keeping a side of his life private from me. Fearing an emotional parting of ways I offered to join Diet in recovery, but he talked me out of it. "You're not an alcoholic, you're just a lush." Soon enough I realized my fear was groundless. Diet quit misdirecting his liquor-fueled anger my way and our relationship actually improved.

Klubstitute had been at The End Up a few months when we heard of a new club space opening in the Haight: Brave New World. On checking it out we discovered a fake-swank olden-style steak house with two rooms, dozens of tables, a professional sound system, and a low, wide stage. It was every-thing we wanted, plus they were offering us Saturday nights! But did the city have enough freaky-fun homos to fill such an enormous space, or were we setting ourselves up for total failure? Diet decided to give it a gamble.

Chapter 25: More Klubstitute

WE SPARKLED LIKE THE RHINESTONES ON a drag queen's
tiara caught in the headlights of a paddy wagon. Activists and
artists, hookers and hustlers, punks, faeries and freaks of
every description showed up dressed for excess and ready to
party at Klubstitutes' Brave New World debut. And they kept
showing up, week after week, crowds of three or four hundred. For alterna-queer San Francisco, this qualified as a
raging triumph. Our goings-on were reported in the gay
papers and even glossy magazines, publicity that sent us into
minor rhapsodies of narcissistic euphoria. We'd arrived!

The only problem was money. Since everyone in our
world was a minor celebrity, the guest list was invariably so
long we made almost nothing at the door despite having
raised admission to a whopping $4.98. I grumbled about
getting paid little more than cab fare, but never considered
quitting. It felt thrillingly novel to be part of something that
wasn't a humiliating failure and might even, with only a
slight stretch of imagination, be considered a public service.
Besides, monetary considerations were far too vulgar a

thing for rarified creatures of The Underground to spend much time thinking about.

With a newly clear head and, spurred by the challenge of a real stage and bigger audience, Diet perfected a cartoonishly exaggerated version of himself as his public persona. His wardrobe grew to include such over-the-top oddities as a floor-length coat of zebra-striped fake fur and pink plastic chaps, his ordinarily jerky movements became positively marionette-like, and his personality went into ironic overdrive. He could clap in a way that suggested the opposite of clapping and roll his eyes in a way that betrayed sincere enthusiasm. His most characteristic movement was a head-bob that excused the audience for not understanding a difficult act but still demanded they appreciate it. Sheer genius. Off-stage he turned into a classic, harried, small-time showbiz promoter—minus the cigar. Picture him pacing around his filthy apartment in a bathrobe while simultaneously yakking loudly on the telephone, eating a sandwich, and making the occasional stab at typing up a press release (that will probably need to be finished and mailed out by yours truly).

And while Diet paced and yakked, I'd be designing flyers, stickers, and posters. Most clubs' promo consisted of modernist graphics and sexy boys. Opting for a campier look, I incorporated kooky images cut from old *Life* magazines or vintage porn rags, then scissored them by hand into fruit shapes, or colored them with day-glow crayons, or sprayed them with adhesive glitter. Then came distribution, which required tramping all over town stapling posters to telephone poles and bulletin boards, leaving flyers in stores, and handing them out at clubs. Klubstitute might only last four hours a week, but it required a day or possibly two of prep work. When the Golden Broom finally succeeded in abolishing street posters it shaved hours of annoying, unpaid labor off my schedule, teaching me a valuable lesson in political irony.

We hadn't been at Brave New World long before we started hearing reports of people getting harassed on the way in. Feeling the need to do something, we posted this notice on the door:

HEY YOU!
This Nightclub & Cabaret is a notorious
Den of polymorphous perversity.
Go elsewhere if you are offended by:
Homosexuality
Avant-garde performance art & video
Scrumptious hors d'oeuvres & swanky cocktails
Lewd & Lascivious behavior
Secular liberal humanism
Swinging musical ensembles
Genderbending
or
"The cultural elite"
thank you for your anticipated
co-operation in this matter.
– The management
(or perhaps we should say the "queenagement")

It's unlikely any queer bashers noticed this (one suspects they aren't big readers), but it helped buck up our spirits, which—since few-to-none of us knew how to fight or owned weapons—was all we could really do.

Klubstitute held a lot of contests: Dina Fruit Fly's Ms. Fag Hag Beauty Pageant, Ruby Toosday's Virgin Queen Contest for first time cross-dressers, and even a Faux Queen contest for drag queens born in women's bodies. Also, in the spirit of the gender-blending times, we hosted a wedding during which Justin Vivian Bond "married" drag king Elvis Herselvis. At some point amidst all this gender mayhem, someone organized a bunch of drag queens to perform a parody protest, invading the club with picket signs reading "SISTERHOOD, NOT MISTERHOOD," "WIGS NOT PIGS," "BITCH NOT BUTCH," and "FEMS AGAINST MACHO BUTCH PRIVILEGE." I didn't see the event myself, but years later came across a description of it in a legit academic tome, Judith Halbertam's *Female Masculinity* (Duke University Press, 1998).

Klubstitute was unusual, but far from unique. In San Francisco's cheap-rent days of yore one couldn't spit without hitting some exciting new scene revolving around a club, magazine, cult, urban-farm, theater troupe, art gallery, publishing house, or what have you. Kooky eccentrics with quirky habits and assumed names have been a specialty here since the 19th century (*See:* Emperor Norton). Yet because of The Plague our social dynamic was decidedly *intense.* People *really* paid attention to performers, and performers *really* gave their all, because for many of us *there might never be a next time.* Barriers between subcultures with contrary aesthetics and ideals lowered so that punks could participate in Radical Faerie rituals, politically correct lesbians could laugh at drag shows, and campy theater queens could listen to political rants.

Though we all continued to gossip and put the moves on each other like normal youngsters, we didn't shy from discussing matters with existential heft: Is it better to accept death with philosophical grace or rage against it with punk rock fierceness? How should one's art address grief and mortality? How much of one's time and energy does one owe to friends in need? How much time and energy does one owe to needy strangers belonging to one's geographic or cultural community? Can art persuade society to be more tolerant and compassionate? Who assigns meaning to life and if it's just us, what do we want our lives to mean? How should one honor the dead?

Awfully serious here. Back to *frou frou*!

Decoration was never simple at Klubstitute because Diet insisted on festooning the club with hand-painted banners, tinsel garlands, and giant swaths of fabric (Superman bed sheets, psychedelic throw rugs, swatches of polyester with weird patterns). At one point he even commanded his minions to scour the thrift stores to buy up Dino the Dinosaur plush toys. Asked why, he smiled cherubically and explained: "I admire Dino's enthusiasm." For a couple of years we dragged something like forty-seven Dinos to each and every Klubstitute just so we could leave them around on chairs and tables, then drag them home at the end of the night. Set up and breakdown were an exhausting round of lugging, assembling, taping, dragging, hoisting, and squeezing of junk into resentful taxicabs, but Diet ignored our heartfelt pleas to simplify.

Why did I, and so many others, tolerate Diet's whims of iron? How was it he could persuade almost anyone into doing almost anything? True, he was adept with sarcastic tongue-lashings, but he relied as much on carrot as stick. Even when reading someone to filth, he'd slip in a dose of sincere flattery. And his appetite for listening to other people's problems, no matter how trivial, was inexhaustible. He'd enthusiastically discuss what sunglasses you ought to wear to the supermarket as if the fate of the world hinged on the decision. Plus, he was upbeat. Even in depressing or frightening situations he exuded the wryly amused, self-mocking fatalism of Cary Grant in a 1930s screwball comedy. And people certainly appreciated that he'd happily divulge the most embarrassing secrets about himself (or anyone else) in a manner that implicitly excused an awful lot of human frailty.

Sometimes, though, I suspect Diet's charisma came from the merry twinkle in his eyes. How exactly is it that eyes twinkle? They're just protoplasmic jelly and can't actually give off light as the word twinkle implies. The best they can do, really, is glint reflectively, something individuals have no control over. True, there are muscles around the eye that scrunch up only with a sincere smile, but they don't produce a twinkle. (I've tested this in a mirror.) So how did Diet twinkle his eyes in such a way as to mesmerize friends and strangers alike, seducing us all into his topsy-turvy world of peculiar quests and secret ceremonies?

I have a theory that I am far too skeptical to believe, but not quite rational enough to entirely discount. Diet was, as I've mentioned, of Irish extraction. From the broad plane of his freckled face to his ruddy red hair, his looks made it perfectly clear that he hailed from the land of leprechauns. Might his twinkle have been an optical illusion created by the rapid darting of his eyes as he tried to catch sight of wee faerie folk whispering in his ear? Or, less plausible but even more thrilling, might Diet himself have been a preternatural being, something like, perhaps, a pooka?

For those unfamiliar with Celtic folklore or the excellent Jimmy Stewart film, *Harvey*, the pooka (or púca) is a mischievous, shape-shifting, nature-spirit with the power of human speech. It's indigenous to northwest Europe and, as one might guess, especially common on the Emerald Isle. Pookas are prone to taking humans on "wild rides," and while they enjoy confusing or terrifying people, they're also known to prophesy and offer advice that leads people away from harm. When spurned, however, they can become vindictive. Sounds more than a bit like one Mr. Diet Popstitute, if you ask me.

Chapter 26: We Could Be Heroes . . . or Not

ALONG WITH THE EPIDEMIC OF AIDS came a secondary epidemic of heroic volunteerism. Hospice volunteers cleaned up diarrhea and vomit, held hands with the dying, and comforted the bereaved. Other volunteers went into dangerous neighborhoods to run needle exchange programs or handed out safe sex info and condoms on street corners. Still others staffed organizations helping find homes for pets orphaned by AIDS, provide support for HIV-positive artists, or make sense of the confusing morass of treatment information. Everyone in gaydom ended up doing *something*, if only small favors for afflicted members of their queer "chosen families." Such favors could be as mundane as doing the dishes or picking up meds at the pharmacy, or extravagant and odd . . . Daisy Chainsaw's loved ones were charged with distributing his ashes to friends in tiny clear bottles filled with glitter and plastic babies after he died.

I felt guilty for not signing up with a do-gooding organization, but told myself that helping run Klubstitute, which occasionally held fundraisers for such organizations, was at least something. I may have shirked my moral obligation to volunteer, but I couldn't shirk my duty to visit the dying. I hated such visits both because death depressed and scared me and because I was wretchedly bad at comforting and consoling.

> *Example #1:* Some dying people opted for total denial. Even at death's door they'd be discussing plans for a trip to Spain in two years or wondering about dog adoption. I'd try to maintain a chipper front with them but felt sure they could see the hopeless anguish in my face.

> *Example #2:* Some dying people raged at everyone they felt was letting them down—the government, straight people, their families, their doctors. I tried to rage along with them but felt sure they could see I wasn't as angry as they were and hated me for it. Just to confuse matters, deniers could become ragers, or vice versa, at unpredictable intervals. I found such shifts difficult to navigate and was always worried I'd rage when I should be denying or deny when I should be raging.

Another problem was what to talk about with the bedridden. My natural inclination was to give pep talks. Usually that was fine, but some people hated pep talks. If you told them, "You're tough as old boots, you'll be out of here in no time!" or "I heard that treatment works wonders," they'd snap at you. On the suspicion that some of the snappers secretly wanted or maybe even *needed* pep talks, I always gave them anyway. Then there was the awkward issue of what to say when a dying person asked how I was doing. I felt disgustingly healthy and reasonably happy, but sharing such info seemed insensitive, so I'd make noises about being busy and share gossip I hoped wouldn't remind the dying person he'd been cut off from the social swirl.

The recently-bereaved provided another set of challenges. One fellow I barely knew called me up after his best buddy died and invited me to be his friend. I really liked him, but never took him up on the offer because his very existence reminded me that I might lose Diet, paralyzing me with icy panic. Other friends who'd lost loved ones started getting a little too into drugs and booze. Was it my place to say anything? I decided not, because I was a louche lush myself, why would they listen to me? On the whole, I found it easier to socialize with people who were dying or bereaved if I put my own feelings on hold. I can't describe the exact nature of the psychic operation I used to squelch my emotions because it happened on instinct, but it got easier as time went on. By the dawn of the nineties I simply became an automaton when confronted with manifestations of mortality.

Chapter 27: Ouch!

I WOKE UP FEELING WOOZY. THERE was a white curtain around my bed, as if I were in a hospital. Why would I be in a hospital? The last thing I remember was . . . what? Standard memory bank search procedures turned up nothing. I glanced down at the floor. White linoleum. I was in a hospital. I sat up and my memory creaked into action. I'd been flown to New York for a weeklong headline gig at The Show Palace Theater, a Times Square strip club.

They'd put me up in a bed and breakfast with chocolate mints on the pillow and flowers in the foyer. This cozy gentility contrasted sharply with the theater itself, a decrepit place full of grubby, grabby men who were incredulous I wouldn't trick with them. Headliners did five shows a day one hour apart, so I'd spent a whole week trapped in the star dressing room (think broom closet) off of the main dressing room. The regular dancers, mostly Black or Latin kids, were always giving me fish-eyed glares, which I interpreted as understandable resentment of my white skin privilege (they never got to headline). At the end of the week I was paid with a big wad of rubber-banded cash like a mafia hit man or a drug runner. I pocketed the money, took one last look at my name up on the grimy white plastic marquee overlooking 8th Avenue, and thought to myself, *Now for some fun!*

Fun meant nightlife, and a few hours later I'd gone out with friends. There'd been drinks and dancing at The Pyramid and . . . my memory conked out again. I reached over to peel back the curtain around my bed and called out to the first passing nurse, an efficient-looking blonde woman in a pale blue uniform.

"Uh, hello?" My voice sounded funny and I couldn't feel my mouth.

The nurse came over to my bedside. "Good morning. Glad to see you're up."

"Why am I in a hospital?"

"You came in an ambulance last night. Your friends said you were attacked. Apparently you were punched in the face. You fell backwards and hit your head."

"I don't remember anything."

She nodded. "You must've gotten a concussion. Also, your jaw is broken. The doctor will come by later to give you a full rundown. Are you in any pain?"

"No."

"Good, but you'll probably need more painkillers soon. When you do, just buzz."

The nurse left and I wobbled up on my feet and into the bathroom where I looked into the mirror. The lower half of my face was grotesquely swollen. I returned to my bed and spent the next several hours in a *grand mal* freakout during which my memories of what I thought of as "the incident" did not return. Eventually Rob, a friend from the preceding night, showed up and filled me in. We'd been walking past Tomkins Square Park when a gang of young toughs came up and punched one of our party. I screamed, "No, no, no!" at which point they punched me. I fell back and hit my head on the edge of the curb and was knocked out cold. After I'd been loaded into an ambulance the police came and took Rob around in a squad car looking for the perps. They didn't find them, but they did find another victim of the same crew, also gay. So although my assailants hadn't specified why they attacked, it was obviously a queer bashing.

Shortly after Rob left, a youngish doctor wearing round glasses came to my bedside. "I'm Dr. Murphy and I'll be operating on you. There's nothing to worry about. Just a broken jaw we can fix right up with a metal plate. But before we operate, I do have a question." He put on a pained smile. "Are you a gay?"

This caught me off-guard. "Why do you ask?"

"Well, if I'm going to be operating on you . . . you could have AIDS and I don't want to get infected."

"You're not planning to share my bodily fluids, I hope!"

Dr. Murphy's pained smile vanished. He looked disgusted. "You can't be too careful."

Absolutely right, I thought. A quick getaway was clearly in order. My return flight was scheduled for that night and Hell, high water, or homophobes, I'd be on it. I hobbled up to the nurses' station, signed papers stating I was leaving "against medical advice," dressed, and left the hospital. I cabbed to my hotel to collect my suitcase, cabbed to the airport, flew home, cabbed to my apartment to drop off my suitcase, then cabbed to SF General. After a few centuries on a gurney under bright fluorescent lights I went into surgery where doctors bolted together my jawbone without a word about my sexual orientation. Rather annoyingly, my mouth had to be wired shut for five weeks afterward, so I couldn't chew solid food. Ravenously hungry, I drank gallons of smoothies but remained unsatisfied till I discovered that it *is* possible to blenderize super chicken burritos if you leave out the tortillas.

A few months after the incident I was walking down Valencia Street with some friends when a bunch of guys in a van driving past yelled out their window at us. "Faggots!" Obeying primal instinct I sprang after the van and caught up with it at the next traffic light. In a mindless fury I pounded the door while jumping around and shrieking, "Come out here and say that to my face!" The van guys rolled up their windows, declining my challenge. The light changed and they drove off.

My rational mind reemerged from wherever it had been hiding to wonder what had just happened. I couldn't subdue a pair of Girl Scouts armed with only a box of Thin Mints let alone beat up a van full of loutish young men armed with lord knows what all. Clearly, I'd been in a fugue state resulting from incident-related brain trauma. Subsequent verbal assaults produced no such reactions, so my loss of impulse control was only temporary. I did undergo one permanent change, though. Post-incident, my political convictions went from firm to intemperate. When I opined that some bigot should be drawn and quartered or cast into a pit of serpents, I jolly well meant it.

Chapter 28: Seven New Types of Sadness

1. The half-sadness mixed with shame of losing someone whose loss should make you very, very sad but only makes you a little bit sad.

2. The relieved sadness of losing someone who'd been suffering to the point where he became angry or cruel and you didn't really want to be around him any more.

3. The *schadenfreude* sadness of losing someone you liked, but whose success or beauty made you jealous.

4. The scary sadness of losing someone with whom you'd once had unprotected sex.

5. The mean sadness of losing someone you hated, but not quite enough to wish him dead.

6. The lackluster sadness of losing someone when you've recently used up the bulk of your sadness on other people's deaths.

7. The frustrated sadness of losing someone you'd always wanted to sleep with, but now never would.

Chapter 29: Sick & Twisted Players

IT STARTED THE NIGHT TONY VAGUELY dragged a discarded Christmas tree in off the street and into Klubstitute for use as a prop in an impromptu recreation of the capsizing scene from the all-star 1970s nautical disaster movie, *The Poseidon Adventure*. The show was such a success he went on to do scenes from movies like *Carrie*, *The Stepford Wives*, *Rosemary's Baby* and dozens more. These quickly evolved into full-scale productions with costumes, cardboard sets (notorious for falling down mid performance), and pre-recorded sound effects. Tony became the director, producer, set designer, and promoter of his own theatrical troupe, The Sick & Twisted Players, while a recurring roster of local actors like Deena Davenport, Omewenne, Michael G. Page, Seanetta AllSass, Don Baird, Q-pid, and others too numerous to list became notorious in his productions.

Tony's shows were spoofs, but he always added clever twist that elevated them above easy parody. He put a brilliantly demonic "Danse Macabre" into *The Exorcist*, replaced cast members who failed to show up with inflatable sex dolls or puppets, handed out 3-D glasses so audiences could see *The Omen* in "Satanivision," and pioneered the theatrical mash-up with shows like *A Very Brady Friday the 13th, Texas Chainsaw 90210*, or *The Fog* starring the cast of *Gilligan's Island*. Like the best drag, his shows mocked rigid gender divisions beloved by Hollywood with some roles played straight (you should pardon the expression), others done in comedic drag, and yet others performed by gender-deviants who didn't mine their cross-dressing for shtick. Gender anarchy in action!

After a couple of years, the Sick & Twisted Players outgrew Klubstitute and began performing at Bernice Street Theater—perfect since it was a warehouse space and Tony could indulge his penchant for splashing the audience with water and fake blood. He also put on shows at professional spaces like The New Conservatory Theater and Life on The Water, way up at super-respectable Fort Mason. At this last spot I did tech for *Carrie* while Tony played the title role of a luckless teenage girl with a crazy religious mom and peers so spiteful, she's forced to slaughter them using her telekinetic powers. The show was hilarious, but Tony wisely left in a bit of the original story's pathos. As he walked slowly across the stage wearing a pink prom dress drenched in fake pig blood his face wore an expression so forlorn it nearly moved me to tears.

Twice, I tried my hand at directing and producing plays with The Sick & Twisteds. First was a dragtacular parody-homage to overwrought 1950s lesbian pulp novels. The show ran at a tiny theater in the living room of a loft-dwelling collective called The Diesel Cathedral and audiences howled with laughter. Emboldened by success, I tried my hand once more, staging a send-up of the hilariously horrid 1960s

teensploitation flick, *The Cool Ones,* starring Connie
Champagne and Johnny Kat, with choreography by Marilyn
Fowler. The premise was that a dancer on a musical variety
show who wants to be a singer breaks out of her go-go cage
and wrestles the mic from the guest star on live TV. She's
fired, but wouldn't ya know it, the crazy kids all think her TV
tussle was a brand-new dance! She becomes a star but *blah,
blah, blah,* gives it up for love. That play, too, was well received,
but I still decided to give up theater. Due to my nervous dispo-
sition the traditional "butterflies in the stomach" before each
show felt like angry hornets.

The Sick & Twisteds inspired multiple imitators who were
slickly professional, but seldom as inventive or amusing. To
explain why, allow me to offer this short disquisition on retro-
camp, by which I mean the ironical-comical re-consumption
of cultural artifacts from the recent past. The most common
example is the hipster's penchant for wearing vintage fashions
that now look slightly silly or watching old movies in a sardonic spirit, but in major cities one can find people who carry
things further: actors staging old TV shows and movies as
plays, collectors obsessing over vintage lunch-boxes and board
games, DJs spinning tunes from defunct and derided musical
genres. For many, retro-camp is not just a hobby, but a career
and/or lifestyle.

Good retro-camp does two things. First, it rescues trends
that have been unfairly subjected to critical savagery by dull-
witted media thinkologists. It finds the authentic spiritual
uplift in sixties Sunshine Pop and admires the ingenuity (or
flat-out gall) behind low-budget special effects from '50s sci-fi
flicks. Second, it allows people to deprogram themselves from

childhood conditioning by lampooning the reactionary sub-texts of old music and films, mocking hoary tropes like *the heroic male saving a damsel in distress* or *the foolishness of secular eggheads who dismiss supernatural menace.* Young Americans, overgorged on pop culture, yearn for such deconstruction the way overeaters yearn for fizzy water. Good retro-camp is nostalgic, but in a productive way, like cleaning out one's attic.

There is, unfortunately, also bad retro-camp, which asks people to laugh *at* the fashions and sensibilities of yesteryear *just* for being outdated. Its underlying message celebrates conformity and consumption: be up to date or you'll be laughable. It mocks old-time-y special effects for being unconvincing, implicitly valuing high-budget over high-concept, money over cleverness. Even when the adherents of bad retro-camp don outdated fashions or listen to passé musical genres they're laughing *at* these outdated things, not at the amusing fact that they *love* these outdated things. It's smug, safe, and dull, dull, dull.

But lets focus on happy thoughts! The Sick & Twisted Players put on over forty shows that left audiences helpless with laughter and, just incidentally, acted as agitprop for an enlightened gender sensibility.

Chapter 30: Dougie

FULL DISCLOSURE: I WAS SLIGHTLY IN love with Dougie, just like everybody else. Pasty pale, punky, and all of nineteen, he'd appeared out of nowhere and began hanging around the clubs and bars where my friends and I were drinking away The Plague. Dougie was impishly handsome with dark, floppy hair, raspberry-red lips, and a little button nose, but what really did it was his "here comes trouble!" smile, a sort of sideways grin just brimming with lust and anarchy.

Dougie was a runaway hustler without schooling, job, fixed address, or responsibilities—a very young person's idea of Free. A fair number of my pals were escorts, exotic dancers, kept boys, and what have you, but Dougie was the only streetwalker. Despite living in a rough-trade demimonde, he wasn't one of those semi-homeless types you worry about inviting over for fear they'll never leave. People that gorgeous *always* have somewhere to go.

So, this stray feral boy with teen idol looks started trysting with this one here and that one there, and everyone he trysted with got his heart broken. Why? Because Dougie's heart was, like the fellow in that old Shangri-Las song, "out in the streets." He never stayed with anyone long because he was addicted to the glamour of the gutter—the exciting unpredictability of living for the moment and outside the law. Plus, he was forever crushing out on his fellow waifs and strays. This happens more than you'd think. Just because someone is chicken doesn't mean he can't be a chicken hawk too.

Dougie was hot for my handsome roommate, Tyler, and would come to my apartment looking for him at all hours. More often than not, Tyler, who found Dougie's rough edges disturbing, would hide in his room pretending to be out. As a consolation prize, I'd invite Dougie into the kitchen for coffee. We'd sit and sip while he told stories of hopping freight trains, living in squats, hustling the streets, negotiating the social welfare system, and—eventually—dealing with health woes from HIV. I listened to these adventure/ crisis tales with rapt attention and a sympathetic ear. Now and then I'd offer the sensible advice bred into me by my suburban middle-class upbringing: "Gee, maybe you could try getting a job?" Or, "If I were you, I'd have nothing to do with those nasty skinheads!" I felt ridiculous because it was obvious Dougie would never settle down but couldn't help myself. I also couldn't help being jealous that, for all my sympathetic listening and top-quality coffee, Dougie always asked for Tyler first when he dropped by.

Dougie never asked me about myself, but he wasn't as self-involved as that makes him sound. Once, after visiting a *sick* friend at SF General, I wandered onto one of the hospital's outdoor terraces for my 19th nervous breakdown when who should pop out of nowhere but Dougie. He was hobbling on a crutch with a bandaged ankle having embroiled himself in some convoluted street scuffle. I explained why I was there and collapsed onto him sobbing. Dougie held me in his arms and said all the right things until I could compose myself, which took kind of a long time.

Among Dougie's fans was Phillip R. Ford. When Phil turned thirty, we held a drug 'n' drag drenched party for him at Klubstitute. At the height of the evening's debauchery the music stopped and Phil, looking very Liberace-goes-Mod in a loud vintage suit with gaudy gold jewelry, was dragged onto the dance floor. A hundred tipsy club-goers sang "Happy Birthday" while someone wheeled out a gigantic cardboard box painted like a fancy pink frosted cake. At the song's conclusion Dougie popped out wearing nothing but underpants and an irrepressible grin. Phil turned to his audience. "For me?" he said, crossing his arms over his chest and fluttering his lashes. "You *shouldn't* have . . . but I'll take him anyway." Dougie hopped into Phil's arms, whispered something into his ears and off they went. Later, Dougie told me he truly liked Phil and hadn't done it for the money, and Phil told me what Dougie had whispered. "I'm on three hits of acid and I'm all yours!"

Years tumbled by, as they do, and Dougie's dramas began to wear on him. His eyes started looking a little tired and his sideways smile sometimes betrayed a shadow of what might have been self-doubt, or possibly regret. He still asked for Tyler first when he dropped by, but never seemed *too* disappointed when he just got me. Pretty boys who make a life out of being desired are actually quite dependent on pathetic souls (like moi) who're enslaved and ensnared by their beauty. Dougie surely saw in my eyes how smitten I was and appreciated the compliment. Alas, I didn't measure up to his standards and he never asked me for anything beyond coffee.

Except once. It was one of those San Francisco nights when the fog hangs so low you'd think you were under a giant circus canopy and the streetlamps are haloed with fuzzy light. I was trolling around South of Market lookin' for love in all the wrong places when who should I spy, but Dougie. We repaired to a bar to spend a pleasant evening diverting ourselves with lighthearted bonhomie and cocktails. At last call, he shyly leaned over to me and hoarsely whispered, "My HIV's becoming symptomatic. I'm kind of freaking out. Can I stay with you tonight?"

I sat Dougie on the seat of my bike while I stood and pedaled us the mile and a half to my apartment. The ride was exhausting and precarious, but worth it for the thrill of Dougie's hands around my waist. Once safely ensconced in my slovenly room, we threw off our clothes and jumped under the covers. Dougie lay on his side and snuggled his thin body into my arms. His skin felt warm, soft, and inviting. I didn't imagine he wanted sex, but asked anyway. He said "no thanks" and I let it go. In my sleepy-tipsy state I imagined that he was safe with me, that my arms offered him some small bit of protection—an absurd thought that allowed me to drift off instead of just lying there. When I woke the next morning, poor Dougie was drooling on my pillow, his face looking worn and frazzled despite his night of sleep. I noticed he'd gotten matching decorative scars on his shoulders, a modern primitive trend that left me cold. Doesn't life provide enough scars without seeking them out?

On waking, Dougie left without much ado and it was months before we ran into each other again. I was walking along the shabby part of Market Street when I spied a circle of crusty punks sitting on the sidewalk looking hostile and downtrodden. Socializing on cement is highly correlated with obnoxious behavior, so I cut them a wide berth. Even so, a kid wearing stomper boots, camouflage pants, and a grungy black hoodie shot over to me asking for money. Before I could respond, I heard, "Don't spare change my friend!" It was Dougie!

Or was it? I had to look twice because the kid who leapt up from the circle and ran over to give me a hug didn't look like the old Dougie. He'd lost his teeth and had that caved in face people associate with elderly hillbillies. Was it speed? A fight? How do you ask someone about something like that? He wasn't even thirty-years-old and his looks were *gone*. In his place I'd have been *devastated*. Dougie was smiling so I squelched all my dismay and said it was great to see him. We walked for a few blocks as Dougie, cheery as you please, asked after Tyler, Phil, and the old crowd. If he felt sorry for himself, he hid it well.

I didn't expect Dougie to last long after that. Even without the ravages of AIDS he was hardly the type to stick around for middle age with all its tedium, wrinkles, and lower back pain. Just not his style. He wanted to be the frosting on life's cake. Still, when I heard he'd died, it seemed impossibly wrong, like the universe had made a colossal mistake.

Chapter 31: Cheerio, 1994

FOR THE MOST PART DIET BORE his ills stoically. He might rage against his condition, "Stupid AIDS!" or use it to manipulate people a little, "You've got to keep me company while I do laundry, I'm dying!" but he wasn't prone to full-on pity parties. His priorities did change, however. Instead of using his laser-sharp powers of analysis on friends' character flaws or concocting elaborate socio-political theories, he focused on outsmarting the virus—no easy task given the wildly differing claims and contentions surrounding treatment for HIV and the bewildering multiplicity of diseases it enabled.

Some did well with AZT; others called it poison. Vitamin C had its adherents, as did acupuncture, Positive Thinking, and kombucha mushrooms, although the medical establishment declared them quackery. And who could even keep track of all the miracle medicines with those sci-fi names? Fluconozole. Interferon. Ziduvodine. Diet tried to discuss his medical options with me, but I resisted, figuring ignorant advice was worse than none at all. This disappointed him—about which I felt terrible—but my brain just wasn't up to the science. I'd read what a glycoprotein or a retrovirus was and forget thirty seconds later. Besides, if there were some combination of treatments that worked, or even *kind of* worked, wouldn't it be front-page news?

After much consideration Diet opted for combining Western and Eastern medicine, the first doled out by SF General, the second by an Israeli acupuncturist named Erez. Along with the needles, Erez put Diet on a regimen of Chinese herbs. When boiled on the stove to produce curative elixirs they smelled unimaginably bizarre and putrid, like the decaying corpse of some demonic fish monster. Despite the herbs, and a medicine chest's worth of conventional prescriptions, Diet fell prey to a host of minor ailments, two bouts of pneumonia, and one of meningitis. Weak and perpetually uncomfortable, his ability to lead a regular life slipped away. He couldn't drink tap water for fear of Cryptosporidium, couldn't pet kitty cats for fear of Toxoplasmosis, and couldn't make it through the day without a nap. For the first time in his thirty-some-odd years he started trying to take it easy, eat right, and get plenty of rest.

But—of course—he said "yes" when Jennifer Blowdryer invited The Popstitutes to perform in London. She was putting on one of her Smutfests, the sex worker cabaret shows she'd started in order to break taboos and give voice to the voiceless. We'd be performing alongside a variety pack of professional perverts including dominatrixes, drag queens, and a young lady calling herself a "necrophile poet." Jennifer couldn't pay airfare, but I'd recently acquired my first credit card *(wheee!)* and decided a small mountain of debt was a reasonable price to pay for the privilege of serenading the

English public. I could only afford plane tickets for Diet and myself, and wasn't willing to ship props or costumes across the globe, so our show would be pared down to the bare nubbins—but so what? London!

De-boarding the plane at Heathrow I nearly fell to my knees and kissed the ground in a fit of Anglophilia. What a thrill to finally visit the land that had given the world heroes like Mary Poppins, Charles Darwin, Christopher Isherwood, and The Sex Pistols! We made our way to the exit gate, where we were met by our old pal Walter from San Francisco.

Diet and I had actually roomed with Walter for a few months in the early '80s. We'd been looking for a place to live when Jennifer mentioned she knew someone with an open room in his apartment. "He's studying German so he can understand the lyrics on Nina Hagen albums!" she told us, her voice full of awe. Nina Hagen, a German punk phenomenon known for her day-glow tresses, operatic trills, and UFO obsession, was a favorite of ours, so naturally we gave Walter a call. He invited us over for an interview and we bussed to his sparsely furnished two-bedroom on Van Ness. We found the room adequate to our purposes (it was cheap and had four walls) and Walter utterly beguiling.

Though he hailed from Texas, Walter's voice neither drawled nor twanged. Rather, he spoke with the clipped, emphatic precision of an English gentleman. Think Rex Harrison in *My Fair Lady*. And instead of "down-home" manners, he affected a semi-aristocratic formality, wielding phrases like "if you please" and "come what may" with the ease of a society matron from days of yore. Clad in a dated, shabby blazer, dress shirt, and slacks, he might have resembled a comically genteel bum from an old movie if not for his bleached blond flat top hairdo and studded leather accessories.

Walter's idea of a roommate interview was chattering at us nonstop whilst serving strong gin and tonics. In the space of a few minutes he railed against President Reagan's latest horror (failing to recognize Samuel Pierce, the only Black member of his cabinet), rhapsodized over Nina Hagen's new album *Nunsexmonkrock*, and turned his former roommate's willful refusal to eat anything beyond popcorn—a habit that resulted in her leaving the apartment on a stretcher—into a droll story. "She wouldn't even use butter!" he said incredulously. I guess we were good listeners because he invited us to move in immediately. On concluding the deal, we all three tipsily fell into bed. Not for nothing was fornication, in those days, often referred to as "the gay handshake."

Life at Walter's felt like living in a highbrow screwball comedy; every conversation was laden with quips, cinematic allusions, and sardonic commentary on current affairs. Gossip flowed and intrigues flowered, wit became wittier and snacks became hors d'oeuvres. Now and then Walter came home from the bars feeling frisky and I'd somehow wind up in his bed making whoopee. There was never any question of our becoming boyfriends, though, because Walter was (he claimed) in love with some exquisitely angelic and unattainable boy whose name I've forgotten. Galen? Lance? Something noble-sounding.

But I'm telling Walter's story all wrong. You have to see his face. Walter had big crooked teeth and exaggerated, angular features so that when he smiled, you felt like you were being sized up for dinner by a hungry gargoyle. These smiles were integral to his character, essential for softening the sharp wit he unleashed whenever confronted with either the things he despised like selfishness, whining, self-congratulation, and bad manners—or the things he pretended to despise like heterosexuals, children, sex, and virtue.

For example, if I went on a hot date, Walter might grimace and mutter about "base animal rutting" then make The Smile. Or when someone mentioned that AIDS was spreading to heterosexuals, he might say, "Thank God, there are so *many* straight people, they're always getting underfoot." Smile. Not for Walter, the new, politically correct term "living with AIDS." When he got *sick*, he announced the news with a cheery, "Guess what? I'm dying!" After which: The Smile.

Actually, Walter didn't get *sick* until after Diet and I had moved off to another apartment, but we stayed in close touch because he was always at The Stud—and by always, I mean *always*. Walter haunted that tavern the way an uneasy spirit haunts a castle. Any connoisseur of barflies would instantly recognize that he was world-class. Some alcoholics live with shame, denial, or a facade of false good cheer. Not Walter. To drink with him was to find oneself in the company of the joyfully damned. He cackled over his cocktails with a sincere and bitter glee. He knew he was frittering his life away and *delighted* in his dissipation. And because he held himself up to high standards and found himself wanting, that naturally gave him leave to judge others in the same harsh light. You could always count on him to skewer sub-par behavior. I think of him sitting in The Stud one Gay Freedom Day when a few post-parade revelers came in sloppy drunk and caterwauling for the DJ to play Madonna. There was more chance of the sun rising in the west than a DJ forgetting to play Madonna that year, but they were insistent. "Madonna! Madonna! We wanna hear Madonnaaaaa!" Walter glanced up from his fifth G&T with a thoughtful look on his face and quietly mused to himself, "Freedom . . . is not *necessarily* a good thing."

Walter was not romantic, he seldom went on dates or had a boyfriend, but he did eventually fall in love . . . with speed. Amphetamines turn many gay men into sex-crazed zombies incapable of thought or speech, but it had the opposite affect on Walter. With every white line he became more verbal, more sexually repressed, and more disdainful of casual manners and boisterous ways. Given this predilection for politeness, it shouldn't have come as a surprise when he up and moved to England. America was just too rowdy and informal for him.

Once safely ensconced in the United Kingdom Walter married a Scottish lass for citizenship and settled into a tiny, tidy flat near a prison with best name ever: Wormwood Scrubs. There he got *sick*, and speed use became ancient history, but he still drank like a champion and maintained his chipper, unyielding cynicism. Noticeably frail, he started using a cane, but with such flair it looked like a gentlemanly affectation. He also managed to make standing on his head for thirty minutes each day to unclog his lungs (doctor's orders) seem more like an amusing eccentricity than a desperate health measure. Despite his enfeeblement, Walter spent a couple of days tour-guiding Diet and I around various pubs, museums, and points of historical interest. Mostly pubs. He truly seemed more English than the English, who were fast abandoning their adorably stuffy reserve and formality for American-style casual manners and tracksuits.

When it came time for The Popstitutes' show, my nerves went all jangle-y. For the first time ever, it would just be Diet and me on stage with no syncopated chaos to distract the audience. I needn't have worried. The English may just have been manifesting some of their much-vaunted good manners, but the audience clapped enthusiastically at the end of our set. Later that night Diet, who wasn't the least bit kinky, allowed one of the following acts, leather types, to bind him in electrical tape, suspend him upside down from the ceiling, and spin him around as part of an S&M ritual. *Some people,* I thought, *will do* anything *to be on stage.*

The day after our show, Diet woke feeling crummy and decided to stay in bed. By nightfall he was feverish, could barely move, barely breathe. Everything hurt like Hell. Walter and I trundled him into a boxy taxicab and sped across town to the Royal Free Hospital in Hampstead where he was whisked onto a bed without delay or red tape. A doctor rushed in and, after giving Diet a brief exam, took Walter and me into the hall to solemnly impart his diagnosis: Diet's lungs were giving out and it didn't look good.

I spent the next few days alternately sitting by Diet's slumbering side and roaming the hospital halls in a state of nervous distress. On one of my perambulations I discovered the hospital chapel, which was decorated in a kind of groovy-modernist 1960s style that temporarily overcame my deep-seated terror of organized religion. I sank to my knees and beseeched the heavens. It's stupid to want to give someone years from your life, like, OK, I'll die at 50 instead of 70 if he can live two more years. It's absurd to throw yourself on the mercy of a universe that's proved time and again its utter and complete indifference to human suffering. It's insane to think, I'll give up my left arm if he gets another six weeks. It's ridiculous to bargain with gods in whom you have no faith. But it couldn't hurt, right?

Then the doctor announced Diet would pull through. He was still weak and not entirely out of danger, though, so he'd need to stay "in hospital" for a while. Every morning after that I took the train across town to sit with him while he, loopy with painkillers, babble-planned Klubstitute special events. "And we'll put on a musical version of *Breakfast at Tiffany's* with the Solid Gold Dancers . . ." The nurses were always dropping by to chat with us about San Francisco. They'd gotten it into their heads the city was a sort of paradisiacal pan-ethnic Utopian radical gay hippie wonderland and found it slightly fantastical that we actually lived there. We, in turn, found it fantastical that English nurses actually had long chats with their patients.

The highlight of Diet's hospital stay came in the form of a letter from Lauren Bacall. Yes, *that* Lauren Bacall. Tony Vaguely had intercepted her book tour, explained Diet's plight, and inveigled her into signing a get-well card. Diet was tickled pink. The trend of film goddesses descending from the silver screen to comfort their loyal gay fans in a time of crisis is one of the few episodes in human history truly deserving of that overused accolade, *fabulous.* Who'd have guessed the plague would inspire so many grand and glorious stars to raise millions for research, lobby congress, and hold hands with the sick and dying?

After three interminable weeks, the hospital released Diet—not good as new, but not *too* much worse for wear. We had one free day before flying home and decided to spend it browsing the craft and collectable stalls of Portobello Road. Under a chalky white sky, we strolled, window-shopped, and ate curry, or tried to in Diet's case. Nothing too special. We were just heading home when I noticed tears on Diet's cheeks. He was smiling, and I worried he was trying to bravely cover up some new pain or infirmity. "You OK?" I asked, dreading a return to the hospital. Diet turned and I saw his smile was genuine. "I'm fine. I just never expected my last day in England to be *so much fun!*"

We'd barely been back on American soil a month when I heard Walter had died. Only with that dreadful news did it occur to me that I'd loved him.

Chapter 32: Even More Klubstitute

SORTING THROUGH THE MOUNTAIN OF FLYERS from Klubstitute days (now safely in the redoubtable hands of Cornell University) makes it clear I've forgotten heaps of what went on there. The Puppetears of Ecstasy? Schnookumz? Clownflesh? My mind draws a blank. Yet some performances are burned into my memory:

Stephen Maxxxine was a popular bartender, Radical Faerie, and man about town. A striking fellow with long, black dreadlocks, he performed as Diamanda Kali-Hagen, slathering his face with post-apocalyptic make-up and wearing an outfit composed of long, long feathers and tattered black leathers. Thus attired, he sang chant-like dirges by Native American singer/ activist Buffy Sainte-Marie, slowly building in force and fury until he'd tapped into some primordial magick energy that had the audience not just mesmerized, but paralyzed. At his show's climax, Stephen swung a huge bloody cow-bone around over his head with such velocity it made a whistling sound, which combined with his hypnotic music to paranormal effect. The orderly procession of seconds and minutes stopped, whooshing the whole audience into an otherworld. I half-expected the indigenous Ohlone tribes to rise from their graves and reclaimed San Francisco for the First Nations.

With her impassively beautiful features, pale skin, long red hair, and witch-y black skirts, Omewenne Grimstone called to mind a snow queen out of some ancient Nordic saga. She sang enchantingly melancholy dirges, holding each note for an icy eternity, whilst seducing hauntingly ethereal tones out of her harmonium (an antiquated variety of mini-organ). On listening to her, the rapid-fire world of the 20th century faded away and one felt transported to the frozen fields surrounding the mighty fortress of Valhalla. Spellbinding!

And no one could forget statuesque chanteuse, Bambi Lake, a San Francisco legend since her arrival in 1970. Like the early Bowie, Bambi reincarnated frequently. Wearing a kicky 1960s pantsuit she performed a tribute to country singer and ahead-of-her-time feminist, Bobbie Gentry. Dressed in black lace she put on a show dedicated to Weimar Germany incorporating Brecht and Weil sung in German as well as a lot of dreamy numbers made famous by Marlene Dietrich. Another show featured Depression-era songs of sophisticated despair like "Black Moonlight" and "Ten Cents a Dance" that'd been rediscovered by early 1970s "genderfuck" pioneers, The Cockettes. Bambi was *most* amazing, everyone agreed, when she sang her own composition, "The Golden Age of Hustlers," a melancholy number about the lost boys of Polk Street and all the men who got away.

The duo Kiki and Herb consisted of Justin Vivian Bond and Kenny Mellman disguised as a haggardly decrepit piano-and-singer lounge act of the sort one imagines playing dinner theaters in Florida. They performed old standards and pop hits (their version of Bonnie Tyler's kitchtastic power-ballad "Total Eclipse of the Heart" was always a show-stopper), in-between which the allegedly octogenarian singer Kiki DuRane, delivered faux-drunken monologues that had everyone in stitches while Kenny, as the lounge lizard-y Herb, tinkled away on the piano. Not long after their time at Klubstitute they moved to New York and became an over-night success, eventually winning an Obie Award and playing Carnegie Hall!

* * *

DIET AND I ALWAYS GUSSIED UP to MC, but at one point he decided *only* full drag would do. On his command I ran to Community Thrift and bought a few blindingly vivid '60s A-line mini-dresses—gorgeous, if a bit common—and a Coco Chanel-style skirt suit in two shades of florescent pink that was *amaaazing.* I then picked up an acid yellow bouffant wig from a garage sale, plastic jewelry from Walgreens, orange fishnet stockings from Foxy Lady Boutique, and day-glow make-up from Kryolan. Thus attired, I became (drumroll, please) Miss Go-Go Chanel! For a short while this was fun. I've always adored whimsical women's fashion and felt privileged to use my body as a mannequin for displaying what I considered beautiful art. Before long, though, doing drag became a drag. I lacked the patience to let my nail polish dry before using my hands so it always sludged-up, even the lowest heels made me wobbly, and dressing up took a small eternity.

"Diet," I whined, "cross-dressing is *too much work.* I don't wanna."

"You're not cross-dressing, you're doing *drag.*"

"What's the diff?"

"Drag queens put on make-up with their fingers. Cross-dressers use brushes."

"And speaking of make-up, it costs money."

Diet turned solemn. "In prison, the queens don't have make-up and are forced to mash up Cheetos for eye-shadow and stain their lips with cherry Kool-Aid. You should be *thankful* you can just go to the store and buy some."

"Maybe if you paid me more than cab fare . . ."

"The trouble with you is, you don't want to cover up your precious *body*. You want to be a *hot man*." Diet's eyebrows added that wanting to be a "hot man" was the height of banality.

This was true, but irrelevant. I never picked up dates at Klubstitute since I spent all night sequestered in the DJ booth spinning whimsical tunes between acts ("Like disco night at a queer insane asylum" opined one of the gay rags) and playing cassette tapes for drag queens who never—I repeat, *never*—cued them up properly. I whined a little longer but Diet remained unmoved. It took a full *year* of steady grousing before Diet finally gave in and allowed me dress like a boy again.

* * *

As if he weren't busy enough, Diet started a theatrical production company—Playstitute—with Andrew Wood, a tall, dashing Englishman. At my insistence he mostly left me out of this, but one sunny Saturday when I was *just not in the mood* he browbeat me into making programs for his musical tribute, *Sondheimania.* Xeroxing in a copy shop smelling repulsively of toner ink, I finally ran out of codependency. I wanted to do my own thing! I didn't know what that thing was, but it wasn't being Diet's unpaid personal assistant. When I delivered Diet the programs, I told him, in the squeaky voice I get when aggrieved, that I was absolutely and incontrovertibly no longer available for free labor. To my great shock, he just said, "All right, you've done your share," and let it drop. Much as I wished this were evidence of our relationship's increasing maturity, I feared it was just that he was losing the energy to manipulate me.

* * *

IN 1993, FOR REASONS I CAN'T recall, Klubstitute was forced to move again. This time we wound up at the 11th Hour, a smaller club on Market at Van Ness. When that closed, we ended up at the Stud, after which we did time at Paula's Clubhouse, then a warehouse space called Studio 4, then a chic restaurant called Eichelberger's, then The Peter Pan (SF's last "rough trade" bar), then a Berkeley disco called Thunder Bay, then a SOMA dive called Cat's Alley, and finally La India Bonita, a tiny Native American-themed Spanish language drag bar in the Mission. I may have gotten the order wrong, but can you blame me? These moves were necessary because Diet was always running afoul of managers disappointed with bar receipts.

The sad truth was that our crowd, after its peak at Brave New World, was shrinking, shrinking, shrinking. This was due partly to the novelty fading and partly to Diet's inattention. He'd begun slacking off on scouting for new acts, instead relying ever more on San Francisco's near infinite supply of lip-syncing drag queens. I found this dull and annoying. "Why don't you book bands any more," I asked. "Or performance art? What happened to the open mics? To zine nights? To Out of Order? The club is getting *tired*."

Uncharacteristically, Diet didn't respond snappishly, but in a curiously off-hand manner, as if he no longer much cared. "The queens have been supportive of the club from the start. You shouldn't be so down on them."

"And what was up with that queen wearing a pig nose who garbled into the mic like a drunk and knocked it over? If a drag queen plays a bitchy woman, misogynistic audience members can take home the message that all women are bitchy."

Diet parried. "Surely you're not saying *all* representations of oppressed people should *always* be flattering."

I returned the serve. "If a drag queen wants to convey that women become bitchy because patriarchal society embitters them, that's fine. But presenting female bitchiness without context is irresponsible. But I'm not just talking about that pig-nosed queen. A lot of those dragheads are just phoning it in, lip-syncing to lame diva pop or trading in sexual innuendo and potty humor. No wonder attendance is down."

Diet squinched his face as if pained and shut me up with a statement as devastating as it was undeniable. "Attendance is down because half the people we're doing this for are dead."

Chapter 33: Final Curtain: 1995

DIET BEGAN LOOKING EMACIATED, NEARLY FLESHLESS. He quit his job and went on disability, moved into Catholic Charities' subsidized housing, and signed up for meal delivery from Project Open Hand. Deena Davenport, a Klubstitute regular, turned angel of mercy, giving him rides to the doctor and trying to make sure he ate. I tried too, popping over to fix one of the three things I knew how to cook, but it was next to useless. Diet had no interest in food and couldn't keep it down anyway. His doctor prescribed appetite-improving pills, but he just threw them up along with everything else. Medical marijuana wasn't legal yet, but—this being San Francisco—pot was still easier to find than a parking space. It helped.

Along with the pot, Diet also went on antidepressants. He never made peace with death or claimed AIDS was "a valuable learning experience" as some did, but instead of their perpetual glower, his eyes began shining with the limitless forbearance and compassion of a saint in mid-martyrdom. This sort of creeped me out. I loved that he'd given up judging the world so harshly, but he'd become a little too *nicey-nice* to seem like Diet any more. Was his newfound placidity the result of emotional maturity or medication or a bit of each? And if it hadn't arisen organically from his mental evolution, did that make it inauthentic or less valuable? I couldn't decide.

Despite his conversion to niceness, Diet's humor retained what might be termed "an edge."

> *Example #1:* Late night outside some disreputable nightclub Diet asked DJ Don Baird if he ever got really, *really* drunk, like vomiting in the street drunk. Don said "rarely," prompting Diet to offer the sage advice, "Well the next time you find yourself vomiting publicly, between hurls you should yell, 'I'm fat, I'm really, really fat!' so people who see you will think you have an eating disorder."

> *Example #2:* At Wolf Creek, the Radical Faerie Sanctuary, Diet asked Jerry the Faerie if he could take his picture. Jerry said "sure," and Diet pulled out a camera and had Jerry pose, then the camera squirted water all over him. Diet then immediately whipped out a real camera and took a picture of Jerry with water dripping from his hair and face.

As Diet's health declined, his personal magnetism increased. Show up at his tiny, cluttered room and you'd find him lounging on his bed in a regal sloth while chatting on the phone with some queen about her upcoming gig at Klubstitute while Deena painted his nails and some boy leafed through his collection of *After Dark* magazines. It felt like a fun sleepover party. To accommodate those who couldn't hang out with him but wanted to demonstrate their

208

affection, a few of Diet's compatriots and I put together a huge 36th birthday party and tribute show: Tributestitute. It went off without a hitch. Scores of performers played music, recited poetry, sang, and put on skits for Diet's entertainment at the Mission District's venerable Victoria Theater. The show lasted over four hours with no intermission, and Diet just sat there bubbling with pleasure throughout. I'd never seen him happier.

Then my brother called to say my mom was dying. She'd been diagnosed with cancer a couple of years before but, since the doctors hadn't given her a timeline, I'd unconsciously decided she wouldn't get *really* sick until I was done dealing with Diet's death. No such luck. I spent a week with my siblings tending her needs as her bodily functions slowly shut down. Then it was over. Anyone who's lost a conspicuously wonderful mother will know how I felt, and anyone who hasn't . . . well, I hope you never do. Suffice to say, I occupied myself with the usual tasks of bereavement: recollecting the deceased, sobbing uncontrollably, and pointlessly wandering from room to room in a thick fog of psychic agony.

During my mother's final days, Diet began riding the wild stallion of dementia. He still had moments of lucidity, but when delusional, he gained a manic energy that sent him gallivanting around town, glassy-eyed and mumbling. I was too broken up about my mom to go to Klubstitute, but he called up and *insisted* I go as he had a surprise for me. I dried my tears, pulled myself together as best I could, and went down to La India Bonita. I found Diet sitting in the dark, dark bar with a couple dozen die-hards. On seeing me he used his new cane to push himself to his feet and smiled.

"Here, this is for you." He handed me a children's play crown constructed from red and gold cardboard. "King of Clubs," he mumbled. This affectionate gesture touched me, but I very much wanted to hide under my blankets and cry for a few hours, so I thanked him and went home to do just that. As I walked down Valencia Street holding my ludicrous crown I decided, rather firmly, that human mortality was a cruel and unjustifiably evil thing.

A couple of nights later (this would be early August of 1995), just two weeks after my mother died, Diet called me at my evening phone job. "I'm in a lot of pain," he said, his voice weak but clearer than it had been in weeks. "I need my medicine . . ." I bolted from my seat and ran to his apartment. Knocking on Diet's door, I heard him call faintly from inside. "It's open." I entered to find him on his bed lit by a nightlight, his face scrunched with pain. "Morphine. It's over there." He weakly gestured toward the bathroom. I located the bottle and poured him the prescribed dosage. With great difficulty he propped himself up on his elbow and swallowed. "Thanks. I'll be able to sleep now."

"Do you want me to stay?"

He lay back down and closed his eyes. "No, I'll be fine."

I didn't want to go. Ever. I wanted to spend the rest of my life right there with Diet beside me, safe and alive. I may have been hallucinating, but just then I saw the atmosphere in his room effervesce with tiny sparkles of light, as if Tinkerbell had waved her wand and enchanted the place.

"Are you sure? I'm happy to stay."

"No, you should go." His face was already unscrunching.

"But what if you need something?"

His eyes closed. "I'm just going to sleep."

"OK, then. Good night." I hadn't kissed Diet since the night we'd met, but I leaned over and kissed his forehead.

"Good night." His breathing became slow and regular. I stood for another half minute, but he didn't stir so I slipped out the door and walked home.

The next morning, I woke to the telephone ringing portentously. I flew into full panic mode even before picking up. It was SF General calling to say Diet had arrived by taxi a few hours previously and gone straight to emergency. They would've called earlier, but they'd misplaced my number. I frenziedly threw on clothes and ran down to the hospital. I found Diet lying unconscious on a bed with something resembling a vacuum cleaner hose running from a whirring machine straight down his throat. I flagged down a pair of passing nurses who explained Diet's lungs weren't working so he was hooked up to a ventilator. It might look uncomfortable, but he wouldn't feel anything as he'd slipped into a coma shortly after arriving. They were about to take him to the Intensive Care Unit.

I staggered into the hall to breathe. One of the nurses, a youngish woman with an unkempt mane of frizzy brown hair, followed me out. As I leaned against the wall to keep from falling over, she spoke to me in a soft, halting voice. "I saw him once . . . your friend. He read a poem at the Above Paradise." Her eyes grew watery. "He was so clever, so *alive*. That's why I moved here from Ohio. To be with people who *felt* things, people who *thought*. People like *him*." Her voice broke with a sob. "And he was *soooo* funny!" When she joined me in weeping piteously, it was just the gift I needed.

Thereafter I visited Diet every day to hold his limp hand—
nails painted in green and orange stripes—and talk about all
the fun things we'd do once he got out. He never stirred, let
alone spoke, but I knew him so well I heard his half of the
conversation in my head. When not staring at Diet, I'd stare at
the monitor over his bed with lines representing his heart rate
and vital signs. Sometimes I'd try to raise them using mind
power, but to no avail. They did rise once, sharply and for
several minutes, at the exact same time—I later learned—the
Sisters of Perpetual Indulgence were holding a public prayer
for Diet. Make of it what you will that when a pale, black-robed
Roman Catholic priest came by to offer Diet "a very special
prayer," the vital signs just sat there.

Along with constant visitors like Deena and Diet's sister
from Marin, various nightclub people were always dropping
by the hospital. Only one or two people were allowed to visit
at a time, so sometimes there'd be a small crowd in the aus-
tere little waiting room down the hall. Diet's bejeweled,
bespangled, and be-dragged friends contrasted vividly with
the other patients' visitors, especially when Diet's pagan
priestess friend Woolfie showed up with her waist-length green
hair, tie-dye robes, and magical staff of gnarled wood. Every
so often nurses came in with updates on Diet's condition. I
could tell from their smiles they found us amusing, and I
knew the carnivalesque atmosphere would have pleased Diet,
but my spirits were not lifted.

I never lost hope exactly, but I understood. When Erez the
acupuncturist saw Diet and whispered to himself, "This is no
good," I understood he meant, "It's over." When Diet's mother
flew in from Massachusetts and gazed down at him with

infinite sorrow, I understood she was saying "Goodbye." When the doctors discussed Diet's case, I understood their deflated tone to mean, "There's no hope." And when dense shrouds of white fog from the west slowly erased the luminous blue summer sky each afternoon, I understood Nature was reminding me of its unyielding decree that *all things must end.*

Diet had been in the hospital for two weeks when a nurse popped her head into the waiting room and delivered astounding news: "Michael is awake." Diet's sister, Deena, and I raced to his bedside and saw him sitting up with his eyes open. He saw us and brightened in a manner that indicated complete lucidity. We all chirped how glad we were to see him, clasped his hands and kissed his cheeks. He couldn't speak because of the tube down his throat so the nurse handed him a pencil and paper. His brow furrowed with effort as he started to write. A half-scribble later he let the pencil drop and rolled his eyes in a manner that clearly said, "Ha, ha. Isn't it just typical? I can't talk so I try to write and now my fingers won't work!" That Diet was not only conscious, but capable of humor, struck me as miraculous. But then Diet's eyes de-focused and his lids drooped.

"Do you need to sleep now?" asked the nurse. "Do you want us to go?" Diet managed a small nod and she took away the pencil and paper. As we said our good nights, Diet's eyebrows shot up as if to say, "Sorry guys, I'm too exhausted for visitors. Being sick is such a drag, I can't wait to get out of here!" His eyes closed and his face relaxed into what looked like a peaceful slumber. Everyone quietly filed out into the hall, but I hated to go. This might well be my last chance to speak with

Diet *ever.* I desperately wanted to tell him . . . what? We'd been yakking at each other continuously for sixteen years. There was nothing unsaid between us. I left with the others.

It was only a day or so later that Diet's vital signs took a sharp turn for the worse and the doctors decided to turn off the machines. Once again Deena, Diet's sister, and I stood around his bed. Then it was all over, just like that.

Chapter 34: Never Can Say Good-Bye

EVERY NIGHT DIET AND I WOULD hang out at bars, dance at clubs, eat Chinese food, and shop at thrift stores, all the while gossiping and debating the issues of the day. Then I'd wake up, remember he was dead, and start screaming. *Noooooo!* Tony Vaguely, who'd drifted away from me over the preceding year, drifted back so he could hold me in his arms and whisper soothing words during these morning freak-outs. With his help I'd compose myself just enough to trudge through my day. Passing locales where Diet and I had lived out our *folie à deux* raised tormenting memories. The time we put a fake mustache on our pal Dina and snuck her into the gay sex club, the time we dropped acid with two straight boys and spent the night discussing music on their bed, all four of us wearing nothing but underpants. I considered moving to L.A., but each morsel of torment linked me to Diet and made me feel less alone. Besides, I didn't know how to drive. In the evenings I'd go home and collapse on my bed like a puppet without an animating hand. Friends called to ask, "Are you OK?" Sometimes I said "yes," sometimes, "no." It made no difference. They'd wish me well, hang up, and Diet would still be dead.

My supply of *joie de vivre* was so depleted, existence itself became a burden. Suicide was off the table—I'm not the type—but I might've found milder ways to snuff myself out: perpetual inebriation, network television, a low-level office job. I could've moved to the suburbs, abandoned my bohemian pretensions, and reinvented myself as a drunken drone, but killing the Old Me would've erased much of Diet's legacy. I was the chief acolyte of Dietness, the foremost expert on Dietology, the prime exponent of Diet Power. Erasing myself in forgetful normalcy would've inflicted a second death on someone who shouldn't have died in the first place.

A month after Diet died someone (was it me?) put together a memorial service at the Women's Building. Unlike Diet, I'd given up unnatural hair colors a while back, but in his honor I sprayed my hair green for the occasion. Several dozen mourners sat on folding chairs and shared memories, passed around photos, cried. I could barely listen, barely speak—if there'd been a casket I'd have thrown myself on it like an Old Country widow screaming, "Take me with you!" Afterward, the Klubstitute crowd repaired to a nearby apartment. People broke out booze and shared more memories, but before long the conversations wandered and the mood lightened. I sat in my collapsing black hole of solitude and misery feeling incredulous. Really? Life was just going to go on? When people started playing board games, I fled.

The press tributes and obits for Diet were plentiful and gratifying, but my favorite accolade was an elegiac poem by Richard Loranger:

CARPE POPSTITUTE

Smashing through the roofbeams, the
imperious Popstitute doth rise:
his hair tiaras in the sky,
his smile unwinds, his whimsied eyes
glitter in the neon night.
Accessoried and manicured,
impeccably attired he
inspects the city sprawled below:
the frenzied mammals in the streets,
the sweetening sweat of discotheques,
the cries of passion in the living room.
What city quakes before the blooming
rake? What army mambos to
his sirened song? What chaos blurts
his vision through the urgent murk
of day? What new species stalks
the tender light of cabaret?
His smile breaks into a laugh,
a mesmerizing and subaural
roar that penetrates walls and skulls,
throbs through groins and genetic codes,
and passes in a pulsing hum,
an aria of echoes that
divorce the future from its course.
He lifts his favorite finger and
a thousand lovers come at once.

Crashing through the roofbeams, the
intrepid sonofabitch doth rise.
He stops, and looks around the room.
The party rages on. He blows
a kiss, and with a bow (no doubt),
he takes his leave, and shuts the door

behind. Thrice a nightbird screams.
Every dancer in the world stands still.
A long silence, a dripping sink,
paper rustling at the door.
Somewhere unutterably far
a lone star cracks in the night.
Then someone howls, and everyone howls,
and everyone stands on the tables and howls,
and all the radios turn on at once,
every music plays at once,
every song is sung at once,
every heart beats at the same
time————aurora borealis
hits a million-mirrored moon
and the lights are UP, the stars careen
around the telepathic hive,
every scrap of polyester
comes alive, all the dogs
dance in the streets, all the flowers
bloom in a cacophony,
billions of pigeons become balloons
and drift into the light, and, for
a moment, everyone can fly.

It would've helped me a lot if I'd gotten a few more dinner invites, phone calls, and check-ins from friends. It's possible I didn't because nobody liked me and I'd only ever been included in the social swirl as Diet's sidekick. It's also possible that condoling social invitations were in short supply due to an overabundance of people in mourning, not to mention the enormous and widespread burden of caring for the *sick*. Whatever the case, I felt abandoned, which made me resentful, which made me feel guilty, which made me angry . . . all of this on top of being really, really sad. Fair to say I wasn't much fun to be around.

* * *

I'D ASSUMED THAT KLUBSTITUTE WOULD BE allowed to
die a dignified death along with Diet, but the queens who'd
predominated over the last couple years started something
called "Klubstitute: The Next Generation." I went once or
twice but there were no drunken poets, no underage punk
bands from Berkeley, no crazy performance artists, just drag,
drag, drag. I tried to explain the club's original eclectic vision
to the organizers, but they stared right through me. I decided
not to make an issue of it. Who was I to put the kibosh on
people honoring Diet's memory in their own way?

Then some Klubstitute regulars decided to hold a parade on
Diet's birthday, February 13th. "Remember, don't wear black!"
said one of the organizers cheerily. I asked why and she looked
at me as if I were dense. "Diet *hated* black clothing." This threw
me for a loop. Diet wore plenty of black . . . though maybe not
toward the end. Then it hit me. Like the Next Generation
queens, the parade crew remembered only late-stage Diet. To
them he was a benevolent jester whose sole wish was for everyone
to dress outlandishly and do saucy, sexy, funny things on stage.
On the day of the parade I woke up feeling as if I were encased
in molasses. The world was dark, thick, and difficult to move
through. I showed up at the agreed meeting point an hour late
and utterly failed to join in the celebratory spirit. We marched
somewhere I guess (I've blocked the memory) and I left as soon
as I could politely escape. The bitter, artsy, intellectual, politi-
cized Diet I'd adored was being forgotten; the iconoclast was
being turned into an icon.

About a year after Diet died, news spread that a combination of protease inhibitors (please don't ask me what that

means) called "the cocktail" was proving effective against the virus. It wasn't "The Cure," but pretty close. Some people couldn't tolerate the drugs and nobody knew how long they'd work, but AIDS was on its way to becoming a manageable condition. That Diet had just missed this reprieve flooded me with despair and, for the first time, guilt. Maybe if I hadn't taken him to England he'd have lasted a little longer and lived. Maybe if I'd cooked for him more often, or helped him formulate a treatment plan . . .

I had neither a benevolent deity nor the promise of afterlife to console me, but I did have something. Just before Diet died, I'd joined forces with Deena Davenport to open a Wednesday night dance club at the Casanova on Valencia Street: Baby Judy's. We decorated with cardboard cutouts—flowers that glowed under black light inside, a six-foot tall Richard Scarry-style bunny rabbit outside—and hired the *crème-de-la-crème* of local freakdom to serve *hors d'eouvres* and go-go dance on the AstroTurf-covered pool table. For tunes we spun lounge, bubblegum, punk, glam, disco, local queer bands like Pansy Division and Enrique, and of course, lots and lots and lots of new wave. We wanted to create a space for lighthearted frolic, somewhere guys could bring a gal pal or wear a silly hat. Somewhere to take people's minds off the plague.

To our surprise, Baby Judy's became a line-out-the-door success. Each week a couple hundred people paid three dollars to cram into the tiny bar to dance, chat, and laugh, laugh, laugh. They laughed because Deena and I couldn't mix to save our lives. They laughed because someone in a green wig and paisley granny dress was offering them a cauliflower floret with blue cheese dip. They laughed because although the grim specter of death roamed the countryside slaying indiscriminately, we were gloriously and deliriously *young and alive*. During the four hours Baby Judy's raged each Wednesday I stockpiled just enough *joie de vivre* to last the rest of the week. My grief was not cured, but it became a manageable condition.

I also discovered that certain songs evoked Diet in certain ways and my record collection became a filing system for feelings. I played "Everything's Gone Green" by New Order when I wanted to feel he was right beside me on a crowded dance floor. I put on "Souvenir" by O.M.D. to recall sitting in his bedroom to have a heart-to-heart at three in the morning. When I needed to let myself feel his absence I played "The Room Nobody Lives In" by Mama Cass and sobbed inconsolably. I don't know why this helped, but it did.

There was, however, another problem for which I had no solution. Without Diet to bounce ideas off and talk things over with, my mind was cast adrift on an open sea of thought . . . and the waves were getting choppy. I'd lost track of where Diet left off and I began. All my opinions had been formulated to interest and amuse him. Were they really even my own? And now that pleasing Diet wasn't an option, what did I want to do with myself? Who the hell was I? For the first time in my adult life, I'd have to decide that without assistance. Diet's death had left me not just alone, but free. Horribly, horribly free.

Chapter 35: Last Dance

EVERYONE KNOWS STRIPPING IS A YOUNG man's game. Sure, a few genetically gifted types stay svelte and sexy into middle age, but I wasn't going to be one of them. At thirty-four I was already manifesting the decrepitude typical of elderly Eastern European Jews: The corners of my mouth sagged downward, giving me a permanently disappointed look; my body began storing fat against the threat of long, brutal Russian winters; dark, world-weary circles appeared under my eyes; my shoulders slumped as if weighted down by countless centuries of anti-Semitism. I was starting to look more *oy, oy, oy* than *ooh, la, la*. Soon I'd have to quit stripping or face the humiliation of getting fired.

I thought about acquiring some new job skills, but somehow, I could never find the energy. Might I have Chronic Fatigue Syndrome? Had I survived The Plague only to be struck down by another viral predator? Then I remembered, oh right, *aging*. Oldsters are always tired. This will grow worse and worse until finally I'm sitting in a chair somewhere gazing vacantly out a window wondering if Joe and Morty are coming over for pinochle later. Actually, retirement sounded quite appealing—until I looked around. Even in my little circle of freaky queens and anarcho-punks I saw conspicuous signs of worldly success. San Francisco's queer underground was, for some, less of a community than a reverse finishing school where kids from dull middle class backgrounds acquired a few interesting rough edges before assuming their place in the larger world . . . publishing books on small presses, teaching at community college, selling their art at minor galleries. Some people I knew were even buying second-hand cars, acquiring health insurance, and vacationing abroad! Far from retiring, my peers were entering their prime.

I needed a "real" job, but who would hire me? True, I'd graduated Phi Beta Kappa from a good university, but the work experience section of my resume—nightclub DJ, tele-marketer, exotic dancer—was that of a louche and feckless scatterbrain. I couldn't type, cook, or drive a car, held no trade-license, spoke no foreign languages, knew nothing of computers, and was bad at math. Stripping, once fun, began making me feel anxious and *un*-Glamorously Doomed. It didn't help that I'd gotten fired from The Nob Hill Cinema in a generalized purge and switched back to the more downscale Campus Theater, its undecorated matte black interior looking like nothing so much as a set for *No Exit* or some other bleak, existentialist drama.

More disturbing yet, some Campus dancers were starting to let customers take forbidden liberties, and some customers were starting to expect the privilege. Those of us intent on retaining privacy for our privates were forced to become increasingly assertive. Improper suggestions were becoming more common as well. "I'm from Iowa, and we don't have places like this one here, no Siree. I always drop by when I'm in town on business. Wanna come back with me to my hotel?" My answer to such queries was always a cheerful "No thanks." It wasn't only that I'd had bad luck with prostitution; the men depressed me. How could they enjoy sex, or even a commercialized simulation thereof, with someone who was only in it for the money? For me the validation of being wanted was key to arousal. Having to pay would've crushed my self-esteem and killed my sex drive.

But then . . . I was working the audience for tips, sliding down the aisle from lecher to lecher with my mind a thousand miles away, when I came across a pair of guys just a whisper over twenty. They wore the generic discount clothes of guys who aren't trying to look hip or sexy: ill-fitting jeans, schleppy shell jackets, grubby sneakers. Both were chatty whilst pawing me, which I found cute because of their thick New Yawk accents. "We tink you're real sexy!" said one. "Dats a great dance you do up dere!" said the other. The first was chunky, the second a string bean, so I mentally nicknamed them Ralph and Ed after the Jackie Gleason and Art Carney characters from *The Honeymooners*. After my show I saw Ralph and Ed in the lobby heading my way. They were whispering back and forth and giving each other little shoves.

"Ask him, ask him!"

"No, you ask him."

"Nuh uh, *you* do it."

"No way, *you*!"

It felt weird realizing they saw me as an intimidating, worldly whore. Couldn't they see that underneath my brash exterior I was just another kid? Finally Ralph, with blushing cheeks no less, screwed up enough courage to ask, "Wouldja wanna do a private show for us?" Now, The Campus had a room in the basement where enterprising dancers were allowed to take customers for . . . well, pretty much *whatever.* Don't ask. Don't tell. Normally I made no use of the space, but I've always had a huge thing for hapless naïfs.

"Ok," I said. "Follow me."

I led the boys down a steep flight of steps to the basement, past the pool table, past the darkened sex maze full of glory holes, and through the door to the private room. To call the space skuzzy doesn't do it justice. This was a crypt-like den of Dickensian squalor. The furniture-free space was tiny, about six by nine feet, and illuminated by the glare of a single, uncovered light bulb. The dank walls were hewn from solid rock while the floor was bare cement. The air smelled earthy and fetid, like the exhalation of some subterranean beast, and one could hear the intermittent whoosh of wastewater from the rusty old pipes crisscrossing the ceiling. If not for the fakey-fake sex moans and hyper-repetitive disco from the movies being screened upstairs one might easily believe oneself to have wandered into an antechamber of Hell.

The boys, unfazed by the ghastly surroundings, handed over some cash (I forget how much, but not much) and we began to mess around. Ralph took one side of me, Ed the other, and they shared the middle. Somehow this all felt innocent and playful, like what might happen at a Boy Scout sleepover. I was just thinking that perhaps I wasn't too old for stripping after all when Ralph and Ed leaned away from me and whispered to each other.

"You got the money?"

"Sure, sure."

"Ask him!"

"No, *you* ask him!"

Finally, Ralph popped the question. "Wanna go back wit us to our hotel?"

I was about to say yes, but stopped because the boys were suddenly breaking my heart. I could see they loved each other the same way Diet and I had, with the unspoken, everlasting affection of Best Buddies. They were a pair of kooky kids on a crazy caper, eternal losers who could never really lose so long as they had each other. Grief chilled my bones and my soul let out an inconsolable wail. I worried the boys would spot my sorrow and start seeing me not as a Sex Object, but a Lonely Guy—something my vanity would never allow. I regretfully declined their offer and went home alone.

After that, The Campus became intolerable. Seeing Ralph and Ed as human accidentally demolished the emotional wall I'd erected between my audience and myself. I'd barely known it was there, but that wall had allowed me to not feel the sadness hiding below the sexy surface of stripping. Once it was gone, I'd gaze out from the stage to see a sea of faces belonging to real men with real needs. Some, I knew, were more or less happily coupled and just looking for a little treat on the side. Others (you could see it in their eyes) were lonely, perhaps trapped in the closet, unhappily partnered, or widowed by plague. They yearned for connection and all they got was a simulacrum of sexiness. It's unrealistic to hope for a world where sex always walks hand-in-hand with intimacy, but does it really belong in bed with commerce?

Thanks to a few thousand dollars inherited after my mom died and Baby Judy's, I was temporarily—for the first time ever—out of paycheck-to-paycheck penury. Before my finances reverted to their usual dire state (or the theater noticed I'd transitioned from Twink to Troll and fired me), I took the step I'd dreaded for so very long and quit stripping forever.

Chapter 36: Still Here

WHOOOOSH! THAT WAS THE SOUND OF all the fabulosity draining out of queerdom. By the mid '90s the continuous demonizing of homosexuality by right-wing bumpkins and religious nuts finally embarrassed educated secular progressives out of their own homophobia. As a result, the walls of prejudice surrounding the ghettos crumbled and gays began skipping out singing, "We're free to be conventional!" Meanwhile closeted gays, already a rather conventional bunch, began coming out in droves. This, along with the inevitable waning of AIDS activism that accompanied the waning of AIDS, tipped the zeitgeist decisively toward normalcy. A few lefty radicals tried to hector everyone into staying marginal in the name of solidarity with the downtrodden, but to no avail. Most gays were perfectly fine with the queerdom being a consumer preference rather than a countercultural community.

This change killed off a lot of the small alternative nightclubs, including Baby Judy's. The new mainstream gays didn't much care for whimsy and went in for an unforgivably terrible brand of dance music so generic they just called it "dance music." Miserable due to the loss of my sole source of happiness, I tried to start more clubs—Monster Island, Hormone Hotel, and Club Analog—but they all flopped. Realizing I was hopelessly out of tune with the times, I reluctantly bid adieu to my DJ career.

I also bid adieu to the old Klubstitute crowd. Or maybe they bid adieu to me. I wasn't exactly a fun person to be around just then, what with the Diet-shaped void following me around everywhere. Or maybe it was just that the Klubstituters and I had always been different species. They were Show Folks who socialized in large groups given to glib wit, glitzy drag, air kissing, and gossip. I, meanwhile, pined for the meandering tête-à-tête gab sessions I'd enjoyed with Diet during which we cackled over amusing ironies and explored all manner of quasi-ludicrous theories. Whatever the case, since I had no new crowd to join, this left me far too alone far too often.

Well, not *totally* alone. I still spoke with Diet frequently, but his sides of our conversations were growing fainter and fainter. This sort of terrified me but I consoled myself with the notion that humans, though we like to think otherwise, are herd animals. Our minds instinctively mirror the thought patterns of those around us. Most likely the parts of my brain in charge of replicating and reflecting Diet's mind were just in the process of integrating with the rest of my neural circuitry. He wasn't so much disappearing as melding into me. Knowing this provided a modicum of theoretical comfort but did not quell my loneliness.

Isolated, depressed, and directionless, I went into a psychic tailspin. The bar has been raised so high for stories of personal disintegration I daren't try to present mine as worthy of note. There were no flirtations with bestiality, heroin, devil worship, or cigars. I just hurled myself into the usual nightlife debauchery, but in a spirit of joyless desperation rather than carefree revelry. I tried good and hard to drown my sadness, boredom, and anomie with physical pleasure . . . and failed. Eventually, after a short bout of "recovery" and a few months with a sliding scale therapist, I decided it was time to sync up with consensus reality and devote myself to a rewarding and useful calling. But what?

* * *

I SAT ON MY LUMPY, UNMADE bed staring out the window as the cement-gray sky drizzled onto an already soggy city. Drip, drip, drip. I had nowhere to go, nothing to do, and no one to meet. Drip, drip, drip. The meaningless patter of falling raindrops lulled me into glum paralysis. Drip, drip, drip. Rain always made me sad, but the perpetual downpour of 1997's "El Niño" put me in an especially dour frame of mind. I felt like one of those stone gargoyles that perch timelessly on the sides of medieval cathedrals.

Then, a miracle. My mind, which had been sluggishly inoperative of late, suddenly conjured a scathingly brilliant idea: I would become a writer! It made *perfect* sense. I'd always been socially awkward, pretentious, moody, self-loathing, judgmental, and besotted with the sound of my own voice. What else *could* I be? As an added plus, I loved reading and adamantly believed literature to be the most civilized (if perhaps not the most effective) means of imposing moral order on a savage and benighted humanity. True, many writers ended their careers broke and bitter, but such a fate held no terrors for me. I was *already* broke and bitter. Given that I hadn't even published yet, one might even say I was *precociously* broke and bitter.

Energized by groundless optimism, I leapt from my bed and sat at my desktop computer. Slowly at first, then faster and faster, I covered its luminous blank screen with words. *Let there be prose!* Out they came, more and more. Electrified vim surged through my fingers, but still they could barely keep up with my racing mind. When I got stuck for a word or turn of phrase, Diet offered suggestions. It felt great to be starting another adventure with him, even if he wasn't really there. On catching sight of my bedside clock, I discovered half a day had passed in what felt like no time whatsoever.

Over the next couple of decades, I churned out a slew of personal essays, one poem, a couple short stories, and three novels. Writing settled my nerves and the bats in my belfry often flapped away for hours at a time. Writing also ended my social isolation (somewhat) by thrusting me into the local literary scene. The people there were brilliant, bizarre, and skittish as cats, but I *adored* them. Soon I had a new social life revolving around open mics, writing groups, book festivals, and reading series. I even got an MFA in creative writing and found work at a bookstore—the first job I ever held, aside from stripping, that didn't feel like torture. I well knew I had as much chance of becoming a Literary Lion as some small-town kid stepping off the bus at Hollywood and Vine had of becoming a movie star, but I couldn't imagine what else to do.

Eventually, time worked its magic on my brain. My memories of the plague years faded to the point where they seemed like a chapter from a history text, like something that had happened to someone else. This distance allowed me to realize I'd never have become my true self if I hadn't separated from Diet and our tiny, cloistered world of jokes and dreams. Despite that, I'd have returned—would still return!—to that world in a heartbeat if somehow miraculously given the chance.

Perhaps a decade passed before my friend Brontez, too young to remember the plague years, asked me something no one had ever asked before. "What was it like when everyone started dying?" I felt my face blanche. My mouth opened, but no words came out. How do you explain what it's like to watch helplessly as your entire world is erased? How do you describe what it's like to lose your soulmate? How do you explain that nothing will ever really be OK again? Finally, I managed to stammer something incoherent involving the words "scary" and "sad." Brontez let the subject drop, but my feeble response shamed me. It also quite appalled the queer phantasms who haunted, and will forever haunt, my mind. That night I began sifting through the jumble of faded images, vaporous impressions, and half-recalled conversations constituting what's left of my memory. Cobbling them into a coherent story wouldn't be easy, but it had to be done, because in so many ways, silence equals death.

Acknowledgements

THE AUTHOR OFFERS HIS UNDYING GRATITUDE to the following for their encouragement and/or assistance: Samuel Ace, Charlie Jane Anders, Jyoti Arvey, Randall Babtkiss, Justin Vivian Bond, Don Baird, Dodie Bellamy, Marke Bieschke, Brian Bouldrey, Katherine Boyle, David Brightman, Peter Carlaftes, Michelle Carter, Nona Caspers, Clint Catalyst, Alexander Chee, Carla Christensen, Robin Clark, Oskar July Cole, Leigh Crow, Drew Cushing, Yvonne Daley, Tim Donnelly, Joe Donohoe, Jacqueline Doyle, Kip Duff, Andrew O. Dugas, Daniel Frontino Elash, Marcus Ewert, Dia Felix, Dan Fine, Phillip R. Ford, Sam Formo, Marc Geller, Kat Georges, Tina Gerhardt, Phoebe Gloeckner, Gravity Goldberg, Wayne Goodman, Sarah Griff, Carrie Hall, Malcolm Hamilton, Trebor Healey, Glen Helfand, Nicole Henares, Luke Heyerman, Johnny Ray Huston, Tyler Ingolia, Jennifer Jazz, Tom Jennings, Tara Jepsen, Jerry the Fairy, Jan Johnson, Jennifer Joseph, Brad Kellogg, Kevin Killian, Zeon Kitchener, Jamie Kitman, Keith Klippensteen, Sam LaBelle, Joy Lanzendorfer, Andrea Lawlor, Ali Liebegott, Beth Lisick, Richard Loranger, MariNaomi, R.J. Martin, Rick May, Toni Mirosevich, Leota Mohr, Carly Nairn, Daniel Nicoletta, Alexander Nowik, Peter Orner, Elissa G. Perry, Beth Pickens,

Brontez Purnell, Kate Razo, Radar Productions, Kirk Read, Larry-bob Roberts, Rob Rosen, Rico Schwartzberg, Austin Seidel, James J. Siegel, Bucky Sinister, K.M. Soehnlein, Cassie J. Sneider, David Henry Sterry, Jenny Stovell, Mattilda Bernstein Sycamore, Michelle Tea, David Jude Thomas, Rose Tully, Scott Upper, Tony Vaguely, Charlie Verrette, Alia Volz, Lewis Walden, James Warner, Gwyn Waters, Jennifer Waters, Sarah Fran Wisby, Marshall Worsham, Eric Zassenhaus, and Olga Zilberbourg.

Photo by Wayne Goodman

About the Author

ALVIN ORLOFF BEGAN WRITING IN 1977, while still a teenager, by penning lyrics for The Blowdryers, an early San Francisco punk band. He spent the 1980s working as a telemarketer and exotic dancer while concurrently attending U.C. Berkeley and performing with The Popstitutes, a somewhat absurd performance art/homocore band. In 1990 he and his bandmates founded Klubstitute, a floating queer cabaret devoted to the ideal of cultural democracy that featured spoken word, theater, drag, and musical acts. In 1995 the club, whose staff and patrons had been ravaged by AIDS epidemic, closed its doors and Orloff suddenly remembered that all he'd ever wanted to be was a writer. He subsequently published three rather whimsical novels, *I Married an Earthling*, *Gutter Boys*, and *Why Aren't You Smiling?* before producing his memoir of life amongst San Francisco's queer underground during the height of the AIDS crisis, *Disasterama!* Orloff currently works as the manager of Dog Eared Books, a literary hot-spot in the heart of San Francisco's Castro District.

Recent and Forthcoming Books from Three Rooms Press

FICTION

Meagan Brothers
Weird Girl and What's His Name

Ron Dakron
Hello Devilfish!

Michael T. Fournier
Hidden Wheel
Swing State

William Least Heat-Moon
Celestial Mechanics

Aimee Herman
Everything Grows

Eamon Loingsigh
Light of the Diddicoy
Exile on Bridge Street

John Marshall
The Greenfather

Aram Saroyan
Still Night in L.A.

Richard Vetere
The Writers Afterlife
Champagne and Cocaine

Julia Watts
Quiver

MEMOIR & BIOGRAPHY

Nassrine Azimi and
Michel Wasserman
Last Boat to Yokohama:
The Life and Legacy of
Beate Sirota Gordon

William S. Burroughs & Allen Ginsberg
Don't Hide the Madness:
William S. Burroughs in Conversation
with Allen Ginsberg
edited by Steven Taylor

James Carr
BAD: The Autobiography of
James Carr

Richard Katrovas
Raising Girls in Bohemia:
Meditations of an American Father; A
Memoir in Essays

Judith Malina
Full Moon Stages:
Personal Notes from
50 Years of The Living Theatre

Phil Marcade
Punk Avenue:
Inside the New York City
Underground, 1972-1982

Alvin Orloff
Disasterama! Adventures in the Queer
Underground 1977–1997

Stephen Spotte
My Watery Self:
Memoirs of a Marine Scientist

PHOTOGRAPHY-MEMOIR

Mike Watt
On & Off Bass

SHORT STORY ANTHOLOGIES

SINGLE AUTHOR

The Alien Archives: Stories
by Robert Silverberg

First-Person Singularities: Stories
by Robert Silverberg
with an introduction by John Scalzi

Tales from the Eternal Café: Stories
by Janet Hamill, with an introduction
by Patti Smith

Time and Time Again:
Sixteen Trips in Time
by Robert Silverberg

MULTI-AUTHOR

Crime + Music: Twenty Stories
of Music-Themed Noir
edited by Jim Fusilli

Dark City Lights: New York Stories
edited by Lawrence Block

Florida Happens:
Bouchercon 2018 Anthology
edited by Greg Herren

Have a NYC I, II & III:
New York Short Stories;
edited by Peter Carlaftes
& Kat Georges

Songs of My Selfie:
An Anthology of Millennial Stories
edited by Constance Renfrow

The Obama Inheritance:
15 Stories of Conspiracy Noir
edited by Gary Phillips

This Way to the End Times:
Classic and New Stories of
the Apocalypse
edited by Robert Silverberg

MIXED MEDIA

John S. Paul
Sign Language: A Painter's Notebook
(photography, poetry and prose)

FILM & PLAYS

Israel Horovitz
My Old Lady: Complete Stage Play
and Screenplay with an Essay on
Adaptation

Peter Carlaftes
Triumph For Rent (3 Plays)
Teatrophy (3 More Plays)

Kat Georges
Three Somebodies: Plays about
Notorious Dissidents

HUMOR

Peter Carlaftes
A Year on Facebook

DADA

Maintenant: A Journal of
Contemporary Dada Writing & Art
(Annual, since 2008)

TRANSLATIONS

Thomas Bernhard
On Earth and in Hell
(poems of Thomas Bernhard
with English translations by
Peter Waugh)

Patrizia Gattaceca
Isula d'Anima / Soul Island
(poems by the author
in Corsican with English
translations)

César Vallejo | Gerard Malanga
Malanga Chasing Vallejo
(selected poems of César Vallejo
with English translations
and additional notes by
Gerard Malanga)

George Wallace
EOS: Abductor of Men
(selected poems in Greek & English)

ESSAY COLLECTION

Womentality: Thirteen Empowering Stories
by Everyday Women Who Said Goodbye to
the Workplace and Hello to Their Lives
edited by Erin Wildermuth

POETRY COLLECTIONS

Hala Alyan
Atrium

Peter Carlaftes
DrunkYard Dog
I Fold with the Hand I Was Dealt

Thomas Fucaloro
It Starts from the Belly and Blooms
Inheriting Craziness is Like
a Soft Halo of Light

Kat Georges
Our Lady of the Hunger

Robert Gibbons
Close to the Tree

Israel Horovitz
Heaven and Other Poems

David Lawton
Sharp Blue Stream

Jane LeCroy
Signature Play

Philip Meersman
This is Belgian Chocolate

Jane Ormerod
Recreational Vehicles on Fire
Welcome to the Museum of Cattle

Lisa Panepinto
On This Borrowed Bike

George Wallace
Poppin' Johnny

 Three Rooms Press | New York, NY | Current Catalog: www.threeroomspress.com
Three Rooms Press books are distributed by PGW/Ingram: www.pgw.com